THE POEMS OF
A. O. BARNABOOTH

Cannes — La Gare

THE POEMS OF
A. O. BARNABOOTH

by Valery Larbaud

TRANSLATED FROM THE FRENCH

BY RON PADGETT AND BILL ZAVATSKY

BLACK WIDOW PRESS
BOSTON, MA

THE POEMS OF A. O. BARNABOOTH by Valery Larbaud. *Les Poésies de A. O. Barnabooth suivi de Poésies Diverses* reprinted by arrangement with Editions Gallimard, Paris. © Editions Gallimard, Paris. English language translation copyright © 2008 by Ron Padgett and Bill Zavatsky. All rights reserved. This is a thoroughly revised version of the original edition published in 1977 by Mushinsha, Ltd. (Tokyo). This book, or parts thereof, may not be reproduced in any form or by any means electronic, digital, or mechanical, including photocopy, scanning, recording, or any information storage and retrieval system, without written permission from the publisher except in the case of brief quotations embodied in critical articles and reviews. For information, contact Black Widow Press, 134 Boylston Street, Boston, MA 02116.

Black Widow Press is an imprint of Commonwealth Books, Inc., Boston, MA. Distributed to the trade by NBN (National Book Network) throughout North America, Canada, and the U.K. All Black Widow Press books are printed on acid-free paper, and glued and sewn into bindings. Black Widow Press and its logo are registered trademarks of Commonwealth Books, Inc.
Joseph S. Phillips, Publisher
www.blackwidowpress.com

Text and cover design by Kerrie Kemperman
Postcards courtesy of Kenward Elmslie and the translators

ISBN-13: 978-0-9795137-9-4
ISBN-10: 0-9795137-9-0

Library of Congress Cataloging-in-Publication Data

Larbaud, Valery, 1881–1957.
[Poésies de A. O. Barnabooth. English and French]
The Poems of A. O. Barnabooth / Valery Larbaud ; translated from the French by Ron Padgett and Bill Zavatsky.
p. cm.
Includes bibliographical references.
ISBN-13: 978-0-9795137-9-4 (alk. paper)
I. Padgett, Ron, 1942- II. Zavatsky, Bill. III. Title.

PQ2623.A65P613 2008
841'.912--dc22

2008021546

Printed by Friesens
Printed in Canada

10 9 8 7 6 5 4 3 2 1

944   NICE. — *Promenade des Anglais.* — LL.

TABLE DES MATIÈRES

I. LES BORBORYGMES

CONTENTS

II. EUROPE

POÉSIES DIVERSES

I. DÉVOTIONS PARTICULIÈRES

II. LA NEIGE

II. EUROPE

VARIOUS POEMS

I. PRIVATE DEVOTIONS

II. SNOW

PREFACE

BY RON PADGETT

There is a country Europe. Now who may be the national poet of Europe?
— Valery Larbaud (1919)

On the fourth of July 1908, a small volume was published anonymous-
ly in Paris in two editions: a hundred review and complimentary copies
with the title *Poèmes par un riche amateur* and another hundred for sale
bearing the title *Le Livre de M. Barnabooth précédé d'une vie de Barna-
booth par X. M. Tournier de Zamble*. The two texts, however, were iden-
tical: a biographical note on the poet A. O. Barnabooth by Tournier de
Zamble, a story by Barnabooth, and the main part, Barnabooth's poems.
The catch was that neither Barnabooth nor Tournier de Zamble existed:
Valery Larbaud had not only written the entire volume, he had paid for
its publication.[1]

Encouraged by the book's favorable response from luminaries such
as André Gide and Octave Mirabeau, Larbaud gradually overcame his
literary reticence.[2] In fact, over the next five years he would become a
friend and sometime traveling companion of Gide, Léon-Paul Fargue,
Francis Jammes, Saint-Jean Perse, Arnold Bennett, Edmund Gosse, and
other writers and editors; he would meet Guillaume Apollinaire and
Joseph Conrad; he would contribute numerous literary essays and arti-
cles to French and English journals; and he would publish one of his
most enduring and popular books, the novel *Fermina Marquez*, which
nearly won the Prix Goncourt.

Thus when the Éditions de la Nouvelle Revue Française published
A. O. Barnabooth, ses oeuvres complètes, in July of 1913, it was with
Larbaud's name on the cover and title page. Eliminated were eleven of
the original poems,[3] Tournier de Zamble's biographical preface, an au-
thor's note, and a smattering of (invented) critical responses. A number
of the remaining poems had been lightly revised; "Europe" (originally
titled "Ievropa") was pared down considerably. A lengthy first-person

Journal intime de A.O. Barnabooth, which Larbaud had been working on since 1905, had been added.[4] This 430-page edition of the poems, the story, and the diary became the standard one that is still in print today.

Tournier de Zamble's preface to the 1908 edition had offered a concise account of the family, life, and character of A.O. Barnabooth. From it we learn that the Barnabooth family line extends back to the Olssons in Finland who, in the seventeenth century, emigrated from Sweden to the Hudson Valley in New York State, where at some point they changed their name to Barnabooth. The most illustrious member of the family was A.O. Barnabooth *père,* an adventurous and enterprising fellow who struck out on his own at age seventeen, crossed the United States, punched cattle, killed a soldier, worked as a miner in Mexico, opened a saloon, went to Central America, worked as a train guard, sailed to Havana, engaged in land speculation, made a fortune, fled a revolution, founded a railway in Lima, gained control of the Peruvian guano industry, amassed a huge fortune that doubled and tripled, sold arms and munitions, and in 1881, at the age of fifty-two, married a sixteen-year-old Australian dancer, Nora May Weller, who, in the unhappy course of their relationship, bore him an only son, in Campamento in the desert province of Arequipa (then part of Chile), on August 28, 1883: Archibaldo Olsson Barnabooth, Jr., the author of these poems.

At the time of his birth Peru, Chile, and Bolivia were warring over the possession of Arequipa, so that technically Barnabooth was born a man without a country. Later he was to become a naturalized American citizen.

At the age of seven A. O.—Spanish and Italian friends called him Archibaldo, English and American friends called him Archie—toured Europe with his father's secretary, returned to South America, and was sent off to a private school in New York. Two years later his father was killed when a gun went off in his face. In yet another accident, Archie's mother died the following year. But long before that he had already been deprived of parental love. After seven years at school he ran away to Europe, living with aristocratic friends in southern Russia and visiting Constantinople, Vienna, Paris, and London. In addition to Spanish and English he was learning German, Italian, modern Greek, and French.

At the age of fifteen Barnabooth fell in love with a beautiful girl five years his senior, Anastasia Retzuch; two years later she became his lover, a liaison that ended with her death. It was then, at the age of twenty, that his inner life surfaced: he grew pensive, read constantly, studied, adopted more sober habits. He placed his stupendous fortune in the hands of competent counsel, purchasing houses and several yachts in order to travel and live conveniently. In London he met and took under his protection two Peruvian sisters, Socorro and Conception Yarza.

Archie's poems, written in French, have now appeared. At twenty-four he is slight, with blue eyes set in a very white face. His health is subject to frequent setbacks. He displays a youthful cynicism born of a disappointment with the world's injustice and hypocrisy, and he often gives forth provocative or contradictory statements that remind one of Lautréamont's *Maldoror*, but sensitivity, compassion, and a lyrical heart are at the basis of his character.

Although Valery Larbaud always dismissed the idea that this persona was a pretext for veiled self-expression, his own biography reads like a parallel but less sensational version of Barnabooth's. He was born in Vichy, France, on August 29, 1881, the only child of Nicolas Larbaud and Isabelle Bureau des Etivaux. Nicolas Larbaud, a pharmacist and the wealthy owner of mineral springs near Vichy, died in 1889 at the age of sixty-seven. From the age of five, an overprotected Valery, whose health was precarious, was taken by his mother to various European spas to convalesce. The happiest years of his childhood were from the age of ten to twelve, which he spent at the Sainte-Barbe-des-Champs boarding school (near Paris), where his contact with children of diverse nationalities encouraged his cosmopolitanism. Language studies, the discovery of contemporary poetry, an interest in geography, trips to the Riviera, a love of books and reading, excursions in France and Spain, then a grand tour of Europe, followed by trips to Italy, further studies, enthusiasm for Whitman, the publication of a small book of poems and another of his translation of Coleridge's *Rime of the Ancient Mariner*, new trips to Switzerland, Germany, and England, disagreements with his mother as to his inheritance, a love affair in the eastern Mediterranean, a return to

France, trips to Belgium, Athens, and Spain, periodic illnesses: the similarities between Larbaud and his persona are evident.[5]

But the concept and modernist style of Larbaud's Barnabooth owe much to the French literature of his time. At the age of nine Larbaud had read Louis Brossenard's *Secret de Monsieur Synthèse*, the story of a man so wealthy he could buy virtually anything, and at fifteen he had been struck by the seeming omnipotence of the very young Roman emperors he discovered in Victor Duruy's *Histoire romaine*. In his adolescence Larbaud had read and admired—in addition to Verlaine and Whitman—Corbière, Rimbaud, Lautréamont, Laforgue, and Wordsworth, as well as the more contemporary Francis Viélé-Griffin, Maurice Maeterlinck, Gustave Kahn, Stuart Merrill, Francis Jammes, Henry Bataille, John Antoine Nau, and Henry J.-M. Levet. Because these last three authors are virtually unknown in the anglophone world, a word on them is in order.

Henry Bataille's book *Le Beau voyage* consists of poems that extol the lyrical beauty of travel, a taste that Larbaud had acquired from the exotic travel romances of Pierre Loti and Jules Verne.

In an essay on John Antoine Nau, Larbaud acknowledged his debt to Nau's collection of poems *Hiers bleus* (1904). Nau, born in San Francisco of French parents (and—shades of Barnabooth and Larbaud—whose father died when John was seven), won Larbaud's admiration by his conversational syntax, his lyricism, his subject matter (often the ocean), and his mystical fascination with the Great Beyond. Appropriately enough, the name Nau was a pseudonym (for Eugène-Léon Edouard Torquet).

In 1902 Larbaud discovered Henry J.-M. Levet's *Cartes postales*, poems that strongly influenced Larbaud's idea of Barnabooth. *Cartes postales* contains ten exotic and sometimes witty poems that Larbaud learned by heart, with lines such as

> La comtesse de Pienne, née de Mac-Mahon
> Se promène sur le boulevard de Mac-Mahon

> (The Countess de Pienne, née MacMahon,
> Strolls along the boulevard de MacMahon)

and

> Ni les attraits des plus aimables Argentines,
> Ni les courses à cheval dans la pampa,
> N'ont le pouvoir de distraire de son spleen
> Le Consul général de France à la Plata!

> (Not the lure of the most attractive Argentines,
> Nor racing on horseback in the pampas,
> Have the power to distract from his spleen
> The Consul General of France in La Plata!)

Because Levet's diplomatic career had taken him through Southeast Asia from Manila to Las Palmas, the exoticism of his poetry is authentic, and he came close to being the poet Larbaud had dreamed of finding, the poet Larbaud describes (in his introduction to Levet's *Poèmes*) as "whimsical, sensitive to racial differences, peoples, countries... very international... humorous... a funny Walt Whitman with a touch of joyous irresponsibility... the successor to Laforgue, Rimbaud, and Whitman."

A nonliterary event also contributed to the formation of the Barnabooth persona. In 1896 Max Lebaudy, a young Frenchman from an extremely wealthy family, died in the army, apparently because the military was over-zealous in showing the rich no favoritism. This made an impression on the young Larbaud, who, like Barnabooth, sometimes felt as if he too were the victim of his wealth: "Alas, I am too rich."

But why, at this point in his writing life, did Larbaud adopt not a pseudonym but a highly developed persona? Previous to *Poèmes par un riche amateur* he had privately published, in very limited editions, three small books: *Les Portiques* (a collection of poems), *Les Archontes, ou la liberté religieuse* (a bogus Greek comedy he purported to have translated, using the pseudonym of L. Hagiosy), and his translation of Coleridge's *Rime of the Ancient Mariner*. The first two volumes he subsequently destroyed and disowned; the third he revised and republished, as he put it, "as an apology to Coleridge and myself." Is it not likely, then, that the persona mask protected Larbaud, during the writing and after the initial publication of the Barnabooth works, from the responsibility of answering for what he wrote? After all, the first edition nowhere bore the name of its true author, and until it received favorable notice from people whose judgment Larbaud trusted, he kept that mask on his face, the one Barnabooth admits to wearing: "I always write with a mask upon my face." What is intriguing in the poems, though, is the way the mask tends, here and there, to slip or dematerialize for a moment, or to melt back into the face it was moulded on. It is this ever-various modulation between cynicism and lyricism, between despair and a love of life, in short, this mercurial involvement of a restless poet fascinated with the mystery of his own identity, that helps make *The Poems of A. O. Barnabooth* the marvelous and modern book that it is.

Larbaud went on to write other charming volumes, of fiction, essays, and memoirs, though, as with the author/persona in *Barnabooth*, the line between these genres would sometimes happily disappear. He also wrote a fifty-page introduction and contributed translations to the best French collection of Whitman's works and helped translate Joyce's *Ulysses* (consulting with his friend the author on this project). Alone he translated volumes by Walter Savage Landor, Arnold Bennett, Samuel Butler, Ramón Gómez de la Serna, and Gabriel Miró. His writing came to an abrupt halt when, in 1935, he suffered a stroke that left him paralyzed on his right side and, for a period of time, mute. When he finally managed to speak, he repeated, several times a day, a sentence that, for people with his affliction (a type of Broca's aphasia), is very rare in its complexity and length: "Bonsoir les choses d'ici-bas" (literally "Good evening, things down here," that is, "Good evening, things of this earth"). Although Larbaud's ability to think and read was not impaired, he never regained verbal fluency, nor was he ever able to write again.

To Larbaud's definitive version of the poems, Bill Zavatsky and I have appended our translation of a curiosity piece and a small group of poems, several of which, aside from their intrinsic interest, reveal Larbaud emerging from the Barnabooth persona. It is not an unexpected transformation. Barnabooth, near the end of his *Diary,* preparing to return to South America and settle down, bids farewell to Europe, farewell to the French language, farewell to his very journal. And in the poem "To Mr. Valery Larbaud" Barnabooth turns, in effect, to his creator and, referring to the poems, asks: "All that, my old Valerio, it's all well and good... But wouldn't there be a way...to leap out of this era?"

In 1957 Larbaud said farewell to life, and now, fifty years later, we are happy to see that more and more anglophone readers are discovering this author who in his own country is considered one of the finest and most innovative writers of the twentieth century.[6] In 1977, when Bill Zavatsky and I published our first version of this translation, I noted how astonishing it was that not a single book by or on Larbaud was in print in English. Since then the situation has brightened considerably. John L. Brown's *Valery Larbaud* is an excellent and compact survey of Larbaud's work. Gilbert Canaan's translation of Barnabooth's diary has been reissued. Larbaud's brilliant meditations on translation, *An Homage to Jerome: The Patron Saint of Translators,* his enchanting collection of stories, *Childish Things,* and his novel *Fermina Marquez* have been published in English for the first time. But his other beautiful pages still await translation.

NOTES

1. Larbaud chose July 4 as the publication date not only because it is the American national holiday but also because it is generally accepted as the date Walt Whitman published the first edition of *Leaves of Grass.* Note also that this is one year before Fernando Pessoa invented the personas of Alberto Caeiro, Ricardo Reis, and Álvaro de Campos. Octavio Paz, in his essay "El desconocido de sí mismo" (1961), makes a case for the probability of Larbaud's influence on Pessoa's use of the heteronym. As for the print run of the first version of *Les Poésies de A. O. Barnabooth,* it might well have been only half the size Larbaud originally declared it to be.

2. Although Larbaud had published his work in magazines a few times under his own name as far back as 1901, he had remained tentative and even timid about presenting his work publicly.

3. These poems were at last reprinted in the Notes section of the Pléiade edition of Larbaud's *Oeuvres* and as an appendix to the Gallimard Poésie edition (1966 and subsequent reprints). During his lifetime Larbaud had refused to allow them to be reprinted. When asked the reason why, he replied, "Not good."

4. The *Journal intime* had appeared in five installments in the *Nouvelle Revue Française* in the months previous to its integral publication in book form.

5. Larbaud's creation of the name Barnabooth is another such point. Tournier de Zamble explains, in his preface, that this unlikely name is made up of the English words *barn* and *booth*—beyond this, he states, its origin is obscure. This bit of faux scholarship amounts to another clever touch to the persona. John L. Brown, in his *Valery Larbaud*, claims that Larbaud invented the name during a stay in London, combining the name of the village of Barnes and that of the English drugstore chain, Booth. Even though the correct name of the chain is Boot's, the explanation is intriguing. Lastly, it is possible that the name was suggested by the *barnabottie*, impecunious eighteenth-century Venetian nobles who rented apartments in what we could call St. Barnaby Street, though of course there was nothing impecunious about Larbaud or Barnabooth. Or was it an oblique reference to the fact that Larbaud's mother controlled the purse strings?

6. In *Enfantines* Larbaud used the interior monologue before he knew of Dujardin or Joyce, and in *Fermina Marquez* he launched the vogue for the twentieth-century novel of adolescence. In general his penchant for erasing the barriers between genres set an example for generations of writers.

ACKNOWLEDGMENTS

For their generous and invaluable help in preparing the initial translation of this volume, we owe a debt of gratitude to the late Vincent Milligan for his close reading, excellent suggestions, and encouragement, and to Serge Fauchereau, for his painstaking checking of the translations and for interpretative readings of the French text. Others who made helpful suggestions or provided information along the way are David Ball, Nicole Ball, Olivier Brossard, Oscar Cerreño, James Coulter, George Economou, Kenward Elmslie, Larry Fagin, Daniel E. Gershenson, Ted Greenwald, Claire Guillot, Rolf Ekart John, Laurence Lang, Anne LeGrand, Pascal Pia, Peter Pouncey, Anne Poylo, George Schneeman, Arlette Smolarski, Chris Tysh, and Richard Zenith. We also owe a debt of gratitude to the librarians at the New York Public Library, especially Alice Hudson of the Map Division, and to John L. Brown, Francisco Contreras, Bernard Delvaille, G. Jean-Aubry, Robert Mallet, Béatrice Mousli, and Frieda Weissman for their scholarly work on the life and work of Valery Larbaud. We also express our appreciation to the magazine editors who first published some of these versions in *Alligatorzine, INTO-GAL, SUN, The World, The Yale Literary Magazine, Vanitas, Washington Square,* and *Z*; to Eric Sackheim, who brought out the first version of this book under the Mushinsha imprint; and to Joseph Phillips, the publisher of the current edition. Finally, we acknowledge the late Kenneth Koch, who one day said to one of us, "Why don't you translate Valery Larbaud?"

—R. P. & B. Z.

LES POÉSIES DE
A. O. BARNABOOTH

THE POEMS OF
A. O. BARNABOOTH

I

LES BORBORYGMES

I

BORBORYGMI

PROLOGUE

Borborygmes! borborygmes!...
Grognements sourds de l'estomac et des entrailles,
Plaintes de la chair sans cesse modifiée,
Voix, chuchotements irrépressibles des organes,
Voix, la seule voix humaine qui ne mente pas,
Et qui persiste même quelque temps après la mort physiologique...

Amie, bien souvent nous nous sommes interrompus dans nos caresses
Pour écouter cette chanson de nous-mêmes;
Qu'elle en disait long, parfois,
Tandis que nous nous efforcions de ne pas rire!
Cela montait du fond de nous,
Ridicule et impérieux,
Plus haut que tous nos serments d'amour,
Plus inattendu, plus irrémissible, plus sérieux—
Oh l'inévitable chanson de l'oesophage!...
Gloussement étouffé, bruit de carafe que l'on vide,
Phrase très longuement, infiniment, modulée;
Voilà pourtant la chose incompréhensible
Que je ne pourrai jamais plus nier;
Voilà pourtant la dernière parole que je dirai
Quand, tiède encore, je serai un pauvre mort «qui se vide!»
Borborygmes! borgorygmes!...
Y en a-t-il aussi dans les organes de la pensée,
Qu'on n'entend pas, à travers l'épaisseur de la boîte crânienne?

Du moins, voici des poèmes à leur image...

PROLOGUE

Borborygmi! Borborygmi!...
Muffled growlings of the stomach and the bowels,
Moans of the flesh endlessly changing,
Voice, irrepressible whisperings of the organs,
Voice, the only human voice that doesn't lie,
That even persists for a while after physiological death...

Darling, so often we have paused in our caresses
To listen to this song of ourselves,
How much it said, sometimes,
While we struggled to keep from laughing!
It rose from deep inside us,
Ridiculous and imperious,
Louder than all our vows of love,
More unexpected, more unpardonable, more serious—
Oh inevitable song of the esophagus!...
Stifled gurgling, liquid glugging from a carafe,
Phrase continuing and infinitely modulated,
The one incomprehensible thing
I can't keep on denying,
The very last word I'll say
When, still warm, I'm a pitiful corpse "clearing itself out"!
Borborygmi! Borborygmi!...
Are they also in the organs of thought
But never heard through the thickness of the brainpan?

At any rate here are poems in their image...

SIBERIA. MANCHURIAN EXPRESS.
(DALNY TO MOSCOW)

ODE

Prête-moi ton grand bruit, ta grande allure si douce,
Ton glissement nocturne à travers l'Europe illuminée,
O train de luxe! et l'angoissante musique
Qui bruit le long de tes couloirs de cuir doré,
Tandis que derrière les portes laquées, aux loquets de cuivre lourd,
Dorment les millionnaires.
Je parcours en chantonnant tes couloirs
Et je suis ta course vers Vienne et Budapesth,
Mêlant ma voix à tes cent mille voix,
O Harmonika-Zug!

J'ai senti pour la première fois toute la douceur de vivre,
Dans une cabine du Nord-Express, entre Wirballen et Pskow.
On glissait à travers des prairies où des bergers,
Au pied de groupes de grands arbres pareils à des collines,
Étaient vêtus de peaux de moutons crues et sales...
(Huit heures du matin en automne, et la belle cantatrice
Aux yeux violets chantait dans la cabine à côté.)
Et vous, grandes glaces à travers lesquelles j'ai vu passer la Sibérie et
    les monts du Samnium,
La Castille âpre et sans fleurs, et la mer de Marmara sous une pluie
    tiède!

Prêtez-moi, ô Orient-Express, Sud-Brenner-Bahn, prêtez-moi
Vos miraculeux bruits sourds et
Vos vibrantes voix de chanterelle;
Prêtez-moi la respiration légère et facile
Des locomotives hautes et minces, aux mouvements
Si aisés, les locomotives des rapides,
Précédant sans effort quatre wagons jaunes à lettres d'or
Dans les solitudes montagnardes de la Serbie,
Et, plus loin, à travers la Bulgarie pleine de roses...

ODE

Lend me your great sound, your great and gentle motion,
Your nighttime glide across illuminated Europe,
O deluxe train! and the heartbreaking music
Sounding along your gilt leather corridors,
While behind lacquered doors with latches of heavy brass
Sleep the millionaires.
I go humming down your corridors
And I follow your run to Vienna and Budapest,
Mixing my voice with your hundred thousand voices,
O Harmonika-Zug!

For the first time I felt all the sweetness of living
In a Northern Express compartment, between Wirballen and Pskov.
We slipped across meadows where shepherds
Under clumps of big trees that looked like hills
Were dressed in uncured, dirty sheepskins...
(Eight o'clock of an autumn morning, and the beautiful soprano
With violet eyes was singing in the next compartment.)
And you, big windows through which I've seen Siberia and the peaks
    of Samnium go by,
Harsh Castile where no flowers grow, and the sea of Marmara under a
    tepid rain!

Lend me, O Orient Express, South-Brenner-Bahn, lend me
Your miraculous and muffled sounds and
Your vibrant trilling voices,
Lend me the light and easy breathing
Of tall slim locomotives, with motions
So free, express locomotives,
Effortlessly leading four yellow cars lettered in gold
Into the mountainous solitudes of Serbia,
And further, across a Bulgaria full of roses...

Ah! il faut que ces bruits et que ce movement
Entrent dans mes poèmes et disent
Pour moi ma vie indicible, ma vie
D'enfant qui ne veut rien savoir, sinon
Espérer éternellement des choses vagues.

Ah! these sounds and this motion
Must enter my poems and say
For me the unsayable in my life,
My stubborn childish life that moves only
Toward an eternal aspiration for vague things.

CENTOMANI

Un détour de la route et ce Basento funèbre,
Dans ce pays stérile, âpre, où, sur des collines,
Au loin, s'étendent de noires forêts pourrissantes.
Sur les interminables plateaux, pas un seul arbre.
Des cirques, des vallées vastes, sans verdure,
Où stagnent, avec des reflets de plomb, des eaux infernales
Issues des crevasses des lointaines montagnes de bitume
Dressées dans les régions désertes, sans routes et sans villages,
Près d'un Lago Nero, où semble demeurer éternellement
Un sombre et angoissant crépuscule d'hiver.
Te voici, rude Lucanie, sans un sourire!
Replis stygiens de ces ravins, ces roseaux noirs,
Ces chemins tortueux ouverts à tous les vents;
J'ai donc vécu, jadis, en Basilicate,
Puisque ces souvenirs me restent bien vivants.

Un détour de la route, et ce Basento funèbre...
(C'est la route de Tito à Potenza;
Ce talus de cailloux, c'est la ligne où ahanent
Les lents and lourds et noirs express Naples-Tarente.)
Il y a une maison de paysan, en ruines,
Inhabitée; sur un des murs on a écrit
En français, ces mots peut-être ironiques: Grand Hôtel.
La prairie, à l'entour, est pâle et grise.
On m'a dit que l'endroit était nommé Centomani.
J'y suis venu souvent, pendant l'hiver 1903.
C'est une partie de ma vie que j'ai passée là,
Oubliée, perdue à jamais...
Arbres, ruines, talus, roseaux du Basento,
O paysage neutre et à peine mélancolique,
Que n'eûtes-vous *cent mains* pour barrer la route
A l'homme que j'étais et que je ne serai plus?

CENTOMANI

A bend in the road and this funereal Basento,
In this bleak and barren country where, on hills
In the distance, dark rotting forests spread.
Not a single tree on these interminable plateaus.
Cirques, vast valleys, not a touch of green,
Stagnant pools with leaden surfaces, hellish water
Leaking from crevasses in distant bituminous mountains
That rise in deserted regions with no roads or villages,
Near a Lago Nero where a gloomy tormenting winter twilight
Seems to dwell eternally.
Here you are, rude Lucania, never a smile!
Stygian meanderings of the ravines, these black reeds,
These winding roads exposed to every wind.
And so I lived there, once, in Basilicata,
Since these memories live deep inside of me.

A bend in the road and this funereal Basento...
(The road from Tito to Potenza:
The slow and heavy and dark Naples-Taranto Expresses
Chug along this rocky grade.)
There's a farmhouse, in ruins,
Abandoned, and on one wall someone has written,
In French, these possibly ironic words: Grand Hotel.
The surrounding plain is pale and gray.
They told me that the place was called Centomani.
I went there often in the winter of 1903.
A part of my life spent there,
Forgotten, lost forever...
Trees, ruins, slopes, reeds of the Basento,
O neutral barely melancholy landscape,
Didn't you have a *hundred hands* to block the way
Of the man I was and will never be again?

Tunisia Palace Hôtel
Veranda - Tea Room

NUIT DANS LE PORT

Le visage *vaporisé* au Portugal
(Oh, vivre dans cette odeur d'orange en brouillard frais!)
A genoux sur le divan de la cabine obscure
—J'ai tourné les boutons des branches électriques—
A travers le hublot rond et clair, découpant la nuit,
J'épie la ville.
C'est bien cela; c'est bien cela. Je reconnais
L'avenue des casinos et des cafés éblouissants,
Avec la perspective de ses globes de lumière, blancs
A travers les rideaux pendants des palmiers sombres.
Voici les façades éclairées des hôtels immenses,
Les restaurants rayonnant sur les trottoirs, sous les arcades,
Et les grilles dorées des jardins de la Résidence.
Je connais encore tous les coins de cette ville africaine:
Voici les Postes, et la gare du Sud, et je sais aussi
Le chemin que je prendrais pour aller du débarcadère
A tel ou tel magasin, hôtel ou théâtre;
Et tout cela est au bout de cette ondulation bleue d'eau calme
Où vacillent les reflets des feux du yacht...
Quelques mois ensoleillés de ma vie sont encore là
(Tels que le souvenir me les représentait, à Londres),
Ils sont là de nouveau, et réels, devant moi,
Comme une grande boîte pleine de jouets sur le lit d'un enfant
    malade...
Je reverrais aussi des gens que j'ai connus
Sans les aimer; et qui sont pour moi bien moins
Que les palmiers et les fontaines de la ville;
Ces gens qui ne voyagent pas, mais qui restent
Près de leurs excréments sans jamais s'ennuyer,
Je reverrais leurs têtes un temps oubliées, et eux
Continuant leur vie étroite, leurs idées et leurs affaires
Comme s'ils n'avaient pas vécu depuis mon départ...
Non, je n'irai pas à terre, et demain

NIGHT IN THE PORT

My face *sprayed* with Portugal
(Oh, to live in this scent of oranges in cool mist!)
Kneeling on the couch in the darkened cabin
—I've turned off the buttons of the electric lights—
Through a clear round porthole that cuts through the night
I spy the city.
This is really it, really it. I recognize
The avenue of casinos and dazzling cafés,
Its perspective of lighted globes, white
Through the hanging curtains of somber palms.
Here are the shining façades of immense hotels,
Restaurants beaming onto the sidewalks, beneath arcades,
And the gilded grilles of the Residence gardens.
I still know every corner of this African city.
Here's the Post Office, and South Station, and I also know
The way I'd go from the docks
To such and such a store, hotel, or theater,
And all of it at the edge of this blue rolling of peaceful water
Where the reflections of the lights of the yacht are shimmering...
Several sunny months of my life are still here
(Just as I remembered them, in London)
Here again, and real, in front of me, now,
Like a big boxful of toys on the bed of a sick child...
And once again I'd see people that I knew
And didn't like, who mean less to me in fact
Than the palms and fountains of the city,
These people who never travel, but who stay
Near their excrement, without ever being bored,
I'd see their once-forgotten faces again, and them
Continuing their narrow lives, with their ideas and their affairs
As if they had stopped living when I left...
No, I'll not set foot on land, and tomorrow

Au lever du jour la «Jaba» lèvera l'ancre;
En attendant je passerai cette nuit avec mon passé,
Près de mon passé vu par un trou
Comme dans les dioramas des foires.

At daybreak the *Jaba* will weigh anchor.
Until then I'll pass the night with my past,
Near my past seen through a hole
As in the dioramas at the fairs.

LE MASQUE

J'écris toujours avec un masque sur le visage;
Oui, un masque à l'ancienne mode de Venise,
Long, au front déprimé,
Pareil à un grand mufle de satin blanc.
Assis à ma table et relevant la tête,
Je me contemple dans le miroir, en face
Et tourné de trois quarts, je m'y vois
Ce profil enfantin et bestial que j'aime.
Oh, qu'un lecteur, mon frère, à qui je parle
A travers ce masque pâle et brilliant,
Y vienne déposer un baiser lourd et lent
Sur ce front déprimé et cette joue si pâle,
Afin d'appuyer plus fortement sur ma figure
Cette autre figure creuse et parfumée.

THE MASK

I always write with a mask upon my face,
Yes, a mask in the old Venetian style,
Long, with a low forehead,
Like a big muzzle of white satin.
Seated at my desk and raising my head
I look at myself in the mirror opposite
Me and three-quarters turned, I see me there,
That childish bestial profile that I love.
Oh, that some reader, my brother, to whom I speak
Through this pale and shining mask,
Might come and place a slow and heavy kiss
On this low forehead and cheek so pale,
All the more to press upon my face
That other face, hollow and perfumed.

OCÉAN INDIEN

Oh, la nuit d'été tropical!
Des atolls d'étincellements émergeant d'abîmes bleuâtres!
Le Crucero flamboyant!
Oh, m'étendre sur le pont d'un grand navire
En route vers l'Insulinde,
Nu, et béer à l'infini béant sur moi.
(Mon coeur d'enfant abandonné, ô cher malade,
Mon coeur serait content de ta main à presser,
Dans cette ombre en feu des nuits
Éblouissantes où je voudrais pouvoir m'envoler.)
Sur les navires d'autrefois, tout pavoisés,
Dont la poupe était un palais aux cents fenêtres dorées,
Et que surmontait un Himalaya de toiles,
On n'avait pas, ininterrompue, cette palpitation des étoiles,
Cette vision de la Création, immensément
Silencieuse—sur la tête, tout déroulé, le firmament.
Je désire un matin de printemps, un peu grisâtre, dans la chambre
    d'hôtel,
La fenêtre ouverte en coin sur la rue de Noailles, à l'air frais,
Et voir là-bas (cinq heures, pas encore de tramways)
Le calme Vieux Port et les bateaux du Château d'If.

INDIAN OCEAN

Oh, tropical summer night!
Atolls of twinklings emerging from bluish depths!
The blazing Crucero!
Oh, to stretch out on the deck of a big ship
On the way to the Dutch East Indies,
Naked and gazing at infinity gazing down on me.
(My childish forsaken heart, O dear invalid,
My heart would be happy just to have your hand to squeeze
In that fiery shadow of dazzling nights
I wish I could fly away in.)
On ships in other times, all decked out,
Whose poop was a palace with a hundred gilded windows
Surmounted by a Himalaya of sails,
They didn't have this uninterrupted starry palpitation,
This vision of Creation, immensely
Silent—overhead, all unrolled, the firmament.
I want a spring morning, a little gray, in my hotel room,
The corner window open on the rue de Noailles, in cool air,
To see over there (five o'clock, still no trolleys)
The calm Vieux Port and the boats of the Château d'If.

NEVERMORE...

Nevermore!...et puis, Zut!
Il y a des influences astrales autour de moi.
Je suis immobile dans une chambre d'hôtel
Pleine de lumière électrique immobile...
Je voudrais errer, à l'aube jaune, dans un parc
Vaste et brumeux, et tout rempli de lilas blancs.
J'ai peur d'avoir d'horribles cauchemars;
Et il me semble que j'ai froid tant il fait clair.
Pcut-être que j'ai faim de choses inconnues?

Ah! donnez-moi le vent du soir sur les prairies,
Et l'odeur du foin frais coupé, comme en Bavière
Un soir, après la pluie, sur le lac de Starnberg,
Ou bien encore les sentiments que j'avais il y a un an,
Regardant de la passerelle de mon yacht
S'ouvrir la baie verte et rose de Gravosa.

NEVERMORE...

Nevermore!...and then, Damn!
There are astral forces around me.
I'm motionless in a hotel room
Full of motionless electric light...
I'd like to wander in the yellow dawn
Through a vast and foggy park
All filled with white lilacs.
I'm afraid of having horrible nightmares,
And it's so light that I seem cold.
Do I hunger for things unknown?

Ah! give me the evening wind on the plains,
And the smell of new-mown hay, as in Bavaria
One evening after the rain on Lake Starnberg,
Or else the feelings I had a year ago,
On the bridge of my yacht watching
The widening green and pink bay of Gravosa.

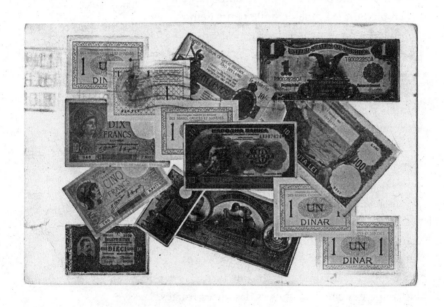

L'ETERNA VOLUTTÀ

Nulle des choses les plus douces:
Ni le parfum des fleurs décomposées,
Ni de la musique en pleine mer,
Ni l'évanouissement bref
De la chute des escarpolettes
(Les yeux fermés, les jambes bien tendues),
Ni une main tiède et caressante dans mes cheveux
M'emplissant le crâne de mille petits démons
Semblables à des pensées musicales;
Ni la caresse froide des orgues
Dans le dos, à l'église;
Ni le chocolat même,
Soit en tablettes fondantes,
Fraîches d'abord puis brûlantes,
Grasses comme des moines,
Tendres comme le Nord!
Soit liquide et fumant
(Hausse vers moi ton baiser lourd, colorada!
Qu'il me pénètre jusqu'à l'essoufflement,
Laissant du feu parfumé après lui
Et une moiteur délicate sur tout mon corps...)
Ni le fumet d'amandes de certains fards;
Ni la vue des choses à travers des vitres rouges,
Ou mauves ou vertes
Comme chez Daniéli, à Venise, au fumoir;
Ni la sensation précieuse de la peur,
Ni le parfum des laques, ni
Les cris matinaux des coqs en pleine ville—
Nul des plus beaux spectacles:
Ni la Méditerranée
Avec son odeur à elle, âcre et bleue,
Avec son froissement et son battement
Si caressants et courts

L'ETERNA VOLUTTA

None of the sweetest things:
Not the scent of rotted flowers,
Not music on the open sea,
Not the quick swoon
Of a dropping swing
(Eyes shut, legs straight out),
Not a warm caressing hand in my hair,
Filling my skull with a thousand little demons
Like musical ideas,
Not the cold caress of organs
At my back, in church,
Not even chocolate,
Be it melting chunks,
First cool then burning,
Fat as monks,
Delicate as the North!
Be it liquid and steaming.
(Lift your sultry kiss to me, *colorada!*
Let it take me until it takes my breath away,
Leaving behind its scented fire
And a light moisture over my whole body...)
Not the almond bouquet of certain cosmetics,
Not the way things look through red windowpanes,
Or mauve or green ones,
As at the Danieli, in Venice, in the smoking parlor,
Not the precious sensation of fear,
Not the scent of lacquers, not
Roosters crowing at dawn in the middle of the city—
None of the loveliest scenes:
Not the Mediterranean
With its special odor, pungent and blue,
With its swishing and slapping
So caressing and quick

Sur les flancs des navires.—
(Oh! nuits sur le pont, quand pas malade, avec l'officier de quart!
Et toi, vigie, ange gardien de l'équipage,
Combien ai-je passé de nuits, silencieux,
A tes pieds, voyant les étoiles dans tes yeux,
Tandis que Boréas nous soufflait au visage.)
Avec ses îles,
Innombrables, diverses,
Les unes blanches avec le gris-vert des oliviers,
Les autres dorées, où l'on aperçoit des villages;
D'autres: de longues choses bleues qui se cachent;
Avec des détroits pleins de musique,
Bonifacio semblable aux portes de la mort,
Messine avec le Faro, Scylla étincelant
Dans la nuit,
Les Lipari avec de rares lumières (une, haute et rouge et coulante);
Et tout le jour
Toute cette mer
Pareille à un grand jardin fleuri...

Non, aucune de ces choses,
Aucun de ces spectacles,
Ne saurait me distraire
De la volupté éternelle de la douleur!
Vous voyez en moi un homme
Que le sentiment de l'injustice sociale
Et de la misère du monde
A rendu complètement fou!
Ah! je suis amoureux du mal!
Je voudrais l'étreindre et m'identifier à lui;
Je voudrais le porter dans mes bras comme le berger porte
L'agneau nouveau-né encore gluant...
Donnez-moi la vue de toutes les souffrances,
Donnez-moi le spectacle de la beauté outragée,
De toutes les actions honteuses et de toutes les pensées viles
(Je veux moi-même créer plus de douleur encore;

On the sides of ships—
(Oh! Nights on the bridge, when not ill, with the officer of the watch!
And you, lookout, guardian angel of the crew,
How many nights have I spent in silence
At your feet, seeing the stars in your eyes
As Boreas blew straight into our faces.)
With its islands
Innumerable, diverse,
Some white, with the graygreen of olive trees,
Others gilded, where villages are glimpsed.
Others: long blue disappearing things,
With straits filled with music,
Bonifacio like the portals of the underworld,
Messina's Faro, Scylla sparkling
In the night,
The Lipari with their few lights (one high and red and flowing),
And all day
That whole sea
Like a great flowering garden...

No, none of these things,
Not one of these scenes
Could distract me
From the eternal voluptuousness of suffering!
You see in me a man
Driven completely mad
By his sense of social injustice
And the world's poverty!
Ah! I'm in love with evil!
I would like to embrace it and become a part of it,
I would like to carry it in my arms the way a shepherd carries
The still sticky newborn lamb...
Let me see all suffering,
Give me the spectacle of outraged beauty,
Of all shameful acts and vile thoughts
(I want to create even more suffering myself,

Je veux souffler la haine comme un bûcher).
Je veux baiser le mépris à pleines lèvres;
Allez dire à la Honte que je meurs d'amour pour elle;
Je veux me plonger dans l'infamie
Comme dans un lit très doux;
Je veux faire tout ce qui est justement défendu;
Je veux être abreuvé de dérision et de ridicule;
Je veux être le plus ignoble des hommes.
Que le vice m'appartienne,
Que la dépravation soit mon domaine!
Il faut que je venge tous ceux qui souffrent
(Et le bonheur n'est pas non plus dans l'innocence);
Je veux aller plus loin que tous
Dans l'ignominie et la réprobation,
Je veux souffrir avec tout le monde,
Plus que tout le monde!
Ne fermez pas la porte!
Il faut que j'aille me vendre à n'importe quel prix;
Il faut que je me prostitue corps et âme;
J'ai si faim de mépris!
J'ai si soif d'abjection!
Et tant d'autres en sont repus; tant d'autres:
Les Pauvres!
Hélas, je suis trop riche; le Mal
M'est à jamais interdit quoi que je fasse:
Je suis un Riche, naturellement bon et vertueux;
Si j'étais plus riche encore, peut-être
Je pourrais acheter la Honte,
Et la douleur et la bassesse toute nue du monde?
Mais que du moins j'entende,
Monter toujours
Le cri de la douleur du Monde.
Que mon coeur s'en remplisse ineffablement;
Que je l'entende encore de mon tombeau,
Et que la grimace de mon visage mort
Dise ma joie de l'entendre!

I want to fan the flames of hatred, burning like a stake).
I want to give contempt a kiss right on the mouth.
Go tell Shame that I'm dying of love for her.
I want to plunge into vileness
As into a very soft bed,
I want to do everything that's rightly forbidden,
I want to be heaped with derision and ridicule,
I want to be the basest of men.
May vice be mine,
Depravity my domain!
I must avenge everyone who suffers
(And there is no happiness in innocence, either).
I want to go deeper than anyone
Into ignominy and reprobation,
I want to suffer with everyone,
More than everyone!
Don't shut the door!
I must go sell myself, the price doesn't matter,
I must prostitute myself body and soul.
How I hunger for hate!
How I thirst for abjection!
And so many others have feasted on them, so many others:
The Poor!
Alas, I am too rich. Evil
Is forever denied me no matter what I do:
I am a Rich Man, naturally good and virtuous.
If I were even richer, maybe
I would be able to buy Shame
And the suffering and the stark naked baseness of the world?
But at least let me hear
The cry of the World's suffering
Rising forever.
Let my heart fill with it ineffably,
Let me still hear it in my grave,
And may the grimace on my dead face
Tell my joy at hearing it!

L'ANCIENNE GARE DE CAHORS

Voyageuse! ô cosmopolite! à présent
Désaffectée, rangée, retirée des affaires.
Un peu en retrait de la voie,
Vieille et rose au milieu des miracles du matin,
Avec ta marquise inutile
Tu étends au soleil des collines ton quai vide
(Ce quai qu'autrefois balayait
La robe d'air tourbillonnant des grands express)
Ton quai silencieux au bord d'une prairie,
Avec les portes toujours fermées de tes salles d'attente,
Dont la chaleur de l'été craquèle les volets...
O gare qui as vu tant d'adieux,
Tant de départs et tant de retours,
Gare, ô double porte ouverte sur l'immensité charmante
De la Terre, où quelque part doit se trouver la joie de Dieu
Comme une chose inattendue, éblouissante;
Désormais tu reposes et tu goûtes les saisons
Qui reviennent portant la brise ou le soleil, et tes pierres
Connaissent l'éclair froid des lézards; et le chatouillement
Des doigts légers du vent dans l'herbe où sont les rails
Rouges et rugueux de rouille,
Est ton seul visiteur.
L'ébranlement des trains ne te caresse plus:
Ils passent loin de toi sans s'arrêter sur ta pelouse,
Et te laissent à ta paix bucolique, ô gare enfin tranquille
Au coeur frais de la France.

THE OLD STATION AT CAHORS

Traveling lady! So cosmopolitan! Now
Shut down, tidied away, retired from business.
Slightly off the beaten track,
Old and pink among the miracles of morning,
With your useless glass roof,
In the sun from the hills you stretch out your empty platform
(This platform once swept
By the dress of air swirling from big expresses),
Your silent platform at the edge of a field,
Your waiting room doors forever closed,
Summer heat crackling the shutters...
O station that has seen so many goodbyes,
So many departures and so many returns,
Station, O double door opening onto the charming immensity
Of the Earth, where God's joy must exist somewhere
Like a thing unexpected and dazzling.
From now on you rest and you taste the seasons
That come back bearing the breeze or the sun, and your stones
Know the cold flashing of lizards, and in the grass where the rails are,
Red and rough with rust,
The light tickling fingers of the wind
Are your only visitors.
The vibration of trains no longer caresses you:
They pass by far away without stopping on your lawn,
And leave you to your bucolic peace, O station calm at last
In the cool heart of France.

VOIX DES SERVANTES

Par la fenêtre ouverte au matin de printemps
(On respire donc un air vivant enfin)! j'entends
Leur voix jeunes emplir la *jaula* sonore...
Ah! pour un moment de joie dans mon cher coeur,
Pour un de ces moments dilatés de santé,
Un de ces moments cruels où l'on est bien soi!
Vivre dans un coin des cent mille replis d'une ville,
Comme une pensée criminelle dans un cerveau,
Et pouvoir acheter tout ce qu'il y a dans les boutiques
Flamboyantes, comme celles de Paris, de Vienne ou de Londres,
Les restaurants, les bijouteries, les rues ouvertes
(L'estomac est une besace pleine, les yeux
Sont deux lanterns allumées).
Vivre donc, oh, de ce matin bleu à ce soir rouge!
Est-ce que je mourrai «un matin de printemps»
Comme celui-là, plein d'air vivant et de chansons?
Oh, mais gonflez mon coeur de vos chansons, servantes!
Voix impériales, voix des filles du Sud!
Énergiques et graves comme les voix des garçons,
Vous vous mêlez à la chaleur et à l'air bleu,
A cette couronne que le soleil pose, là-haut, au mur aigu,
Cette bandelette orangée, aux confins des cieux, et que je vois
Levant la tête vers les abîmes éthérés.

Rythmant le travail, les airs en choeur,
Les vieilles scies, les refrains neufs;
Et les choses sentimentales de toujours:
La «Paloma» et «Llora, pobre corazon»,
Les choses d'il y a dix ans, vous vous souvenez?
«Con una falda de percal blanca...»
(Mon vieux coeur, tous nos beaux matins de la Navé!)
Les zarzuelas de l'an dernier, comme
«El arte de ser bonita» ou «La gatita blanca».

SERVANTS' VOICES

Through the window open to the spring morning
(Breathing living air at last!) I hear
Their young voices filling the resounding *jaula*...
Ah! For a moment of joy in this dear heart of mine,
For one of those expansive moments of health,
One of those cruel moments when one is really oneself!
Living in a corner of a city's hundred thousand folds,
Like a criminal thought in a brain,
Able to buy everything in the dazzling shops,
Like those in Paris, Vienna, or London,
Restaurants, jewellers, wide-open streets
(The stomach like loaded saddlebags, the eyes
Two lighted lanterns).
So to live, oh, from this blue morning to this red evening!
Will I die "one spring morning"
Like this one, filled with living air and songs?
Oh, but swell my heart with your songs, servant girls!
Imperial voices, voices of Southern girls!
Energetic and full-toned as the voices of boys,
You blend with the heat and the blue air,
With that crown the sun places, up there, on the sharp wall,
That orange strip at heaven's borders I see
When I look up into ethereal depths.

Working in rhythm, the chorus of airs,
The good old songs, the new refrains,
And the always sentimental things:
"La Paloma" and "Llora, pobre corazón,"
Things from ten years back, remember?
"Con una falda de percal blanca..."
(Old heart of mine, all our beautiful mornings on la Navé!)
Last year's zarzuelas, like
"El arte de ser bonita" or "La gatita blanca."

Écoutez ces furieuses, criant à grosses voix, l'air:
«Anteayer vi a una señora...»
(Vous vieillirez, refrains, et vous aussi, ô voix
Qui, pures, vous élancez de ces gorges charmantes!)

O servantes de mon enfance, je pense à vous,
Divinités au seuil de la maison profonde,
Bonnes sambas crépues, et vous, cholitas rouges,
Toi, surtout, ma Lola, grande vieille farouche
Avec des yeux fous et durs fixés au loin sur le monde.
Mais c'est toi qu'aujourd'hui je voudrais tant revoir,
Et ravoir (bien plus tard, à Paris, je me souviens)
Toi, Rose Auroy, dans les jardins de l'ambassade,
En rabane rayée et foulard rouge à pois bouton d'or,
Et me disant (je revois tes grands yeux
D'un noir doré, profonds et graves
—Car je t'aimais surtout pour douloureuse et grave)
«Mossié, veut-ti savoi les sirandanes?»
Les sirandanes, milatresse, les sirandanes!
«Mon la maison, l'a beaucoup di fenêtes, une seule pôte?»
Et je cherchais, au fond de tes yeux inoubliables,
Le mot de l'énigme, ô poseuse de sirandanes!
Alors tu disais comme sortant d'un rêve,
Riant soudain: «Dé à coude! Mossié, dé à coude!»
Rose Auroy, te souviens-tu de ce petit garçon exotique
Que la vieille Lola nommait «Milordito»?
O Servantes, chantez! voix brûlantes, voix fières!
Toutes les criadas de la maison, chantez!
Amparo, Carmeta, Angustias, chantez!
Et remplissez ce coeur qui vous dédie ces larmes...

Listen to these madwomen crying in booming voices the melody,
"Anteayer vi a una señora…"
(You'll grow old, refrains, you too, O pure voices
That take flight from these charming throats!)

O servant girls of my childhood, I think of you,
Divinities at the threshold of the deep house,
Frizzy samba maids, and you, red cholitas,
You most of all, my Lola, great old wild woman
With your hard crazy eyes staring into the distance.
But today you're the one I'd really like to see again,
And have again (I remember you from Paris, much later)
You, Rose Auroy, in the embassy gardens,
In streaked raffia and red silk scarf dotted with buttercups,
And saying to me (I see your large eyes
Of dusky gold again, deep and serious
—Because I loved you most for serious and sad)
"Suh, you want to know de sirandanes?"
The sirandanes, mulatto woman, the sirandanes!
"Me house he has lots windows, only one door?"
And deep down in your unforgettable eyes, I sought
The enigmatic word, O poser of sirandanes!
Then as if coming out of a dream you said,
Suddenly laughing, "A thimble, suh! Thimble!"
Rose Auroy, do you remember the exotic little boy
That old Lola named "Milordito"?
O servant girls, sing! Burning voices, proud voices!
All you criadas of the house, sing!
Amparo, Carmeta, Angustias, sing!
And fill this heart that dedicates these tears to you…

MATIN DE NOVEMBRE PRÈS D'ABINGDON

Les collines dans le brouillard, sous le ciel de cendre bleue
Comme elles sont hautes et belles!
O jour simple, mêlé de brume et de soleil!
Marcher dans l'air froid, à travers ces jardins,
Le long de cette Tamise qui me fait songer aux vers de Samain,
Marcher sur la terre de nouveau inconnue, toute changée,
Et pareille au pays des fées, ce matin d'arrière-automne...
O nature voilée, mystérieux paysages, vous ressemblez
Aux blocs des maisons géantes et aux avenues brumeuses de la ville,
Vous avez l'imprécis grandiose des horizons urbains.

NOVEMBER MORNING NEAR ABINGDON

The hills in the mist, under an ash blue sky,
How high and beautiful they are!
O simple day, mingled with fog and sun!
Walking in the cold air through these gardens,
Along this Thames which makes me think of the poems of Samain,
Walking the earth made new again, all changed,
And like a fairyland this late autumn morning...
O veiled nature, mysterious landscapes, you resemble
The blocks of giant houses and the foggy avenues of the city,
You have the grandiose imprecision of urban horizons.

ALMA PERDIDA

A vous, aspirations vagues; enthousiasmes;
Pensers d'après déjeuner; élans du coeur;
Attendrissement qui suit la satisfaction
Des besoins naturels; éclairs du génie; agitation
De la digestion qui se fait; apaisement
De la digestion bien faite; joies sans causes;
Troubles de la circulation du sang; souvenirs d'amour;
Parfum de benjoin du tub matinal; rêves d'amour;
Mon énorme plaisanterie castillane, mon immense
Tristesse puritaine, mes goûts spéciaux:
Chocolat, bonbons sucrés jusqu'à brûler, boissons glacées;
Cigares engourdisseurs; vous, endormeuses cigarettes;
Joies de la vitesse; douceur d'être assis; bonté
Du sommeil dans l'obscurité complète;
Grande poésie des choses banales: faits divers; voyages;
Tziganes; promenades en traîneau; pluie sur la mer;
Folie de la nuit fiévreuse, seul avec quelques livres;
Hauts et bas du temps et du tempérament;
Instants reparus d'une autre vie; souvenirs, prophéties;
O splendeurs de la vie commune et du train-train ordinaire,
A vous cette âme perdue.

ALMA PERDIDA

To you, vague aspirations, enthusiasms,
Thoughts after lunch, emotional impulses,
Feelings that follow the gratification
Of natural needs, flashes of genius, agitation
Of the digestive process, appeasement
Of good digestion, inexplicable joys,
Circulatory problems, memories of love,
Scent of benzoin in the morning tub, dreams of love,
My tremendous Castilian joking, my vast
Puritan sadness, my special tastes,
Chocolate, candies so sweet they almost burn, iced drinks,
Drowsy cigars, you, sleepy cigarettes,
Joys of speed, sweetness of being seated, excellence
Of sleeping in total darkness,
Great poetry of banal things: news items, trips,
Gypsies, sleigh rides, rain on the sea,
Delirium of feverish nights, alone with a few books,
Ups and downs of temperature and temperament,
Recurring moments from another life, memories, prophecies,
O splendors of the common life and the usual this and that,
To you this lost soul.

YARAVI

Dans ce grand souffle de vent noir que nous fendons
Exalté, j'erre en pleurant sur le pont du yacht;
Minuit en mer, pas une côte en vue.
Tout à l'heure au coucher du soleil,
Dans la brume grondaient les canons du Bosphore,
La côte d'Asie à la côte d'Europe répondant
(Pour guider les vaisseaux) de quart d'heure en quart d'heure.
Et c'est avec ces bruits guerriers à la poupe que, bondissant,
Mon navire au nom bouffon, le «Narrenschiff»,
Est entré dans cette nuit de poix et ce chaos du Pont-Euxin...

Encore enfant, j'ai parcouru ce chemin
D'obscurité, ce déroulement du grand flot porphyréen
Tout chargé des livides fleurs d'edelweiss maritime.

O demain! le lever du jour sur les ravages
Et dans mon cher coeur plein de cloches!
A l'infini, les côtes de l'Empire ottoman
Roses et vertes, aux ondulations douces, où se cachent
Des villages couleur de la terre et de vieilles forteresses;
Ou bien l'approche d'un port russe, annoncé
Par des milliers de courges vertes flottant sur l'eau brillante
(Comme l'Ausonie parfois, plus discrètement,
S'annonce au navigateur par un fiaschetto vide que berce
Le flot tyrrhénien).

Oh, les levers du soleil d'été sur les mers retentissantes
Et le silence des ravages vus au loin!

Mais laissez-moi m'attendrir un peu sur mon enfance,
Me revoir à quinze ans dans les rues d'Odessa;
Laissez-moi pleurer dans la nuit sans savoir pourquoi,

YARAVI

In this great blast of dark wind we're cutting through
I wander, exalted, weeping on the deck of the yacht.
Midnight on the sea, no land in sight.
A little while ago at sunset
The cannons of the Bosphorus were booming in the fog,
The coast of Asia answering the coast of Europe
(To guide ships) every quarter hour.
And with these warlike sounds off the stern,
My bounding ship with its farcical name, the *Narrenschiff,*
Entered this pitchblack night and the chaos of the Euxine Sea...

As a child I followed this route
Of darkness, this unrolling of the great porphyrian wave
Bursting with the livid flowers of sea edelweiss.

O tomorrow! Sunrise on the coast
And in my own dear heart full of bells!
The pink and green coasts of the Ottoman Empire stretched out to
    infinity,
With gentle undulations, where villages
The color of earth are hidden, and old fortresses,
Or the approach of a Russian port, announced
By thousands of green gourds floating on the sparkling water
(The way Ausonia, more discreetly, sometimes
Announces itself to the navigator by an empty *fiaschetto* rocking
On the Tyrrhenian wave).

Oh, summer dawns on resounding seas
And the silence of shores seen from far away!

But let me be touched a little by my childhood,
Seeing myself again at fifteen in the streets of Odessa,
Let me weep in the darkness without knowing why,

Et chanter dans le vent ces vers:
«Ya que para mi no vives»,
Sur un air de valse entendu je ne sais où, un air des tziganes,
Chanter en sanglotant sur un air de tziganes!
Le souvenir me fait revoir des pays éblouissants:
Des rades pleines de navires et des ports bleus
Bordés de quais plantés de palmiers géants et de figuiers
Gigantesques, pareils à des tentes de peau pendues aux cieux;
Et d'immenses forêts à demi submergées,
Et les paseos ombragés de Barcelone;
Des dômes d'argent et de crystal en plein azur;
Et la Petite-Cythère, creuse comme une coupe,
Où, le long des ruisseaux les plus calmes du monde,
Se jouent toutes les pastorales du vieux temps;
Et ces îles grecques qui flottent sur la mer...

Je ne saurais dire si c'est de désespoir ou bien de joie
Que je pleure ainsi, mêlant
Mes sanglots étouffés aux cris de panique de l'aquilon,
Au rythme de la machinerie, au tonnerre et au sifflement
Des vagues tordues en masses de verre sur les flancs
Du navire, et tout à coup étalées comme un manteau de pierreries
(Mais tout cela est invisible)...

Mais ma douleur... Oh, ma douleur, ma bien-aimée!
Qui adoptera cette douleur sans raison,
Que le passé n'a pas connue et dont l'avenir
Ignorera sans doute le secret?
Oh, prolonger le souvenir de cette douleur moderne,
Cette douleur qui n'a pas de causes, mais
Qui m'est un don des Cieux.

Singing these lines into the wind:
"Ya que para mi no vives,"
To a waltz melody heard I don't know where, a gypsy melody,
Sobbing as I sing a gypsy melody!
Memory opens onto dazzling countries again:
Harbors full of ships and blue ports
Lined with docks planted with giant palm trees
And gigantic fig trees, like tents made of hide hung from the sky,
And immense forests half-submerged,
And the shady paseos of Barcelona,
Silver and crystal domes against the azure,
And Little Cythera, hollow as a cup,
Where, along the calmest streams in the world
All the old-time pastorals are played:
And those Greek islands floating on the sea...

Whether I weep this way from joy or despair
I can't say, mingling
My stifled sobs with the panicky cries of the North Wind,
To the rhythm of the machinery, the thunder and the hissing
Of waves twisted into masses of glass on the sides
Of the ship, and suddenly spread like a cape of precious jewels
(But all that is invisible)...

But my sorrow... Oh, my sorrow, my beloved!
Who will adopt this groundless sorrow,
Unknown to the past and whose secret
The future will doubtless never understand?
Oh, to prolong the memory of this modern sorrow,
This sorrow which has no cause, but
Which for me is a gift from Heaven.

MERS-EL-KÉBIR

J'aime ce village, où sous les orangers,
Sans se voir, deux jeunes filles se disent leurs amours
Sur deux infiniment plaintives mandolines.
Et j'aime cette auberge, car les servantes, dans la cour,
Chantent dans la douceur du soir cet air si doux
De la «Paloma». Écoutez la paloma qui bat de l'aile...
Désir de mon village à moi, si loin; nostalgie
Des antipodes, de la grande avenue des volcans immenses;
O larmes qui montez, lavez tous mes péchés!
Je suis la paloma meurtrie, je suis les orangers,
Et je suis cet instant qui passe et le soir africain;
Mon âme et les voix unies des mandolines.

MERS-EL-KEBIR

I love this village, where beneath the orange trees,
Two girls, each unseen by the other, speak their love
On two infinitely plaintive mandolins.
And I love this inn, for servants in the courtyard
Sing in the sweetness of evening that sweet song
"La Paloma." Listen to the fluttering paloma...
Desire for my own village, so far away, longing
For the antipodes, for the great avenue of immense volcanoes.
O welling tears, wash away all my sins!
I am the wounded paloma, I am the orange trees,
And I am this passing moment and the African evening,
My soul and the united voices of the mandolins.

VOEUX DU POÈTE

Lorsque je serai mort depuis plusieurs années,
Et que dans le brouillard les cabs se heurteront,
Comme aujourd'hui (les choses n'étant pas changées)
Puissé-je être une main fraîche sur quelque front!
Sur le front de quelqu'un qui chantonne en voiture
Au long de Brompton Road, Marylebone ou Holborn,
Et regarde en songeant à la littérature
Les hauts monuments noirs dans l'air épais et jaune.
Oui, puissé-je être la pensée obscure et douce
Qu'on porte avec secret dans le bruit des cités,
Le repos d'un instant dans le vent qui nous pousse,
Enfants perdus parmi la foire aux vanités;
Et qu'on mette à mes débuts dans l'éternité,
L'ornement simple, à la Toussaint, d'un peu de mousse.

THE POET'S WISHES

When I am dead and several years have passed,
And cabs keep on colliding in the fog
The way they do today (nothing will have changed),
Let me be a cool hand on some brow!
On the brow of someone humming as he rides
Along Brompton Road, Marylebone, or Holborn,
And dreaming of literature, looks on
The tall black monuments in the thick yellow air.
Yes, let me be the sweet dark thought,
The secret thought in the urban noise,
A moment's rest in the wind that pushes us on,
Children lost amid the Vanity Fair.
And for my debut in eternity, let them place
The simple decoration, on All Saints' Day, of a bit of moss.

MUSIQUE APRÈS UNE LECTURE

Assez de mots, assez de phrases! ô vie réelle,
Sans art et sans métaphores, sois à moi.
Viens dans mes bras, sur mes genoux,
Viens dans mon coeur, viens dans mes vers, ma vie.
Je te vois devant moi, ouverte, interminable,
Comme une rue du Sud béni, étroite et chaude,
Et tortueuse entre des maisons très hautes, dont les faîtes
Trempent dans le ciel du soir, heurtés
Par des chauves-souris mou-volantes;
Rue, comme un grand corridor parfumé
D'un Barrio del Mar dont la mer est en effet voisine,
Et où, dans la nuit calme, tout à l'heure,
Les serenos psalmodieront les heures...

Mais, ma vie, c'est toujours cette rue à la veille
Du jour de Saint-Joseph, quand des musiciens,
Des guitares sous leurs capes, donnent des sérénades:
On entendra, jusqu'au sommeil très doux, le bruit
Plus doux encore que le sommeil, des cordes et du bois,
Si tremblant, si joyeux, si attendrissant et si timide,
Que si seulement je chante
Toutes les Pepitas vont danser dans leurs lits.

Mais non!
Mon chant entrecoupé de cris! mon chant à moi!
(Ce n'est pas toi, Amérique, tes cataractes, tes forêts
Où frémit la venue du printemps, ce n'est pas toi,
Grand silence des Andes prodigieux et solitaires,
Ce n'est pas vous, non, qui remplissez ce coeur
D'une harmonie indescriptible, où se mêlent
Une joie féroce et des sanglots d'orgueil!...)
Oh! que j'aille dans les lieux inhabités, loin des livres,
Et que j'y laisse rire et hurler
La bête lyrique qui bondit dans mon sein!

MUSIC AFTER READING

Enough words, enough sentences! O real life,
Artless and unmetaphored, be mine.
Come into my arms, sit on my lap.
Come into my heart, come into my lines, my life.
I see you in front of me, open, interminable,
Like a street in the blessed South, narrow and warm,
Winding between such high houses, whose rooftops,
Steeping themselves in the evening sky, are bumped
By soft-flying bats,
Street like a large fragrant passageway
Of a Barrio del Mar whose neighbor is indeed the sea,
And where, in the quiet night, in a little while,
The serenos will sing out the hours like psalms...

But, my life, it's always this street on the eve
Of Saint Joseph's Day, when musicians,
Guitars beneath their capes, go serenading.
On the brink of a very gentle sleep you'll hear
The sound of strings and wood, even gentler than sleep,
So trembling, so joyful, so touching, and so tentative,
That if only I were to sing
All the Pepitas would dance in their beds.

But no!
Cries interrupt my song! My own song!
(You're not the one, America, your cataracts, your forests
Where the coming spring trembles, you're not the one,
Great silence of the stupendous, lonely Andes,
No, you're not the ones who fill this heart
With an indescribable harmony, mingling
Fierce joy and sobs of pride!...)
Oh! If I could only go where no one lives, far from books,
And let the lyrical beast leaping in my breast laugh and howl!

345 Scheveningen. Gezicht op het strand.

SCHEVENINGUE, MORTE-SAISON

Dans le clair petit bar aux meubles bien cirés,
Nous avons longuement bu des boissons anglaises;
C'était intime et chaud sous les rideaux tirés.
Dehors le vent de mer faisait trembler les chaises.

On eût dit un fumoir de navire ou de train:
J'avais le coeur serré comme quand on voyage;
J'étais tout attendri, j'étais doux et lointain;
J'étais comme un enfant plein d'angoisse et très sage.

Cependant, tout était si calme autour de nous!
Des gens, près du comptoir, faisaient des confidences.
Oh, comme on est petit, comme on est à genoux,
Certains soirs, vous sentant si près, ô flots immenses!

SCHEVENINGEN, OFF-SEASON

In the bright little bar with polished furniture
We lingered over English drinks.
How nice and warm behind these drapes, one thinks.
Outside the sea wind made the chairs chatter.

It was like a smoking lounge on a train or ship:
I was deeply moved, subdued and far away.
My heart was sinking, as if on a trip.
I was like a well-behaved child filled with anxiety.

Still, around us nothing seemed to move,
People whispering secrets at the bar.
O how on our knees, how small we are
Some evenings, with you so near, O immense waves!

THALASSA

Couché sur le divan au fond de la cabine
(Bercé comme une poupée aux bras d'une fillette folle
Par le tangage et le roulis—gros temps),
J'ai sur l'âme un cercle lumineux: le hublot,
Comme une vitrine de boutique où l'on vendrait la mer;
Et, à demi sommeillant, je rêve
De construire, dans une forme inusitée encore, un poème
A la gloire de la mer.

O Homère! ô Virgile!
O Corpus Poeticum Boreale! C'est dans vos pages
Qu'il faut chercher les vérités éternelles
De la mer, et ces mythes qui expriment un aspect du temps,
Et les féeries de la mer, et l'histoire des vagues,
Et le printemps marin, et l'automne marin,
Et l'accalmie qui fait une route plate et verte
Au char de Neptune et aux cortèges des Néréides.

J'ai sur l'âme un cercle lumineux qui voyage
De haut en bas, tantôt empli du bleu-gris moucheté de blanc
Du paysage méditerranéen, avec un coin de ciel
Pâle, tantôt
C'est le ciel qui descend remplir le cercle, tantôt
Je plonge dans une lumière glauque et froide,
Tourbillonnante, et tantôt, d'un seul coup,
Le hublot aveuglé de bave bondit s'éblouir en plein ciel blanc.

Passe, sur cette ligne d'horizon toujours mouvante,
Grand comme un jouet, un vapeur roumain, peint en blanc;
Il roule comme sur un chemin crevé de fondrières, et l'hélice
Sort parfois de la mer et bat l'air plein d'écume.
Ils saluent, du drapeau d'arrière, à mi-mât,
Bleu—jaune—rouge.

THALASSA

Lying on the couch in the back of the cabin
(Rocked like a doll in the arms of a crazed little girl
By the pitch and roll—foul weather),
I have a luminous circle on my soul: the porthole,
Like a shop window where the sea is for sale,
And half-asleep, I dream
Of constructing, in a completely new form, a poem
To the glory of the sea.

O Homer! O Vergil!
O Corpus Poeticum Boreale! Yours are the pages
One must search for the eternal truths
Of the sea, and those myths that express a vision of weather,
And the fairylands of the sea, and the history of the waves,
And ocean spring, and ocean autumn,
And the lull that smoothes a flat green road
For Neptune's chariot and the Nereids' processionals.

I have a luminous circle on my soul that travels
Up and down, sometimes filled with the blue-gray flecked with white
Of the Mediterranean landscape, with a patch of pale
Sky, sometimes
It's the sky that comes down to fill the circle, sometimes
I plunge into a cold and glaucous light,
Swirling, and sometimes, in one fell swoop,
The porthole blinded by froth flies up, dazzling itself in white open sky.

On the ever-moving horizon line,
Big as a toy, painted white, a Rumanian steamer passes.
It rolls as on a road crisscrossed by muddy ruts, and sometimes
The propeller lifts out of the sea and churns the air full of foam.
They salute, with the flag on the stern at half-mast,
Blue—yellow—red.

Bruits du navire: voix dans un corridor,
Craquements des boiseries, grincements des lampes oscillantes,
Rythme des machines, leur odeur fade par bouffées,
Cris mangés de vent, qui brouillent la musique
D'une mandoline égrenant: «Sobre las olas del mar...»
Et le bruit coutumier qui finit par être silence.

Oh! sur le pont, là-haut, le vent long long et féroce, le vent pirate
Sifflant dans les cordages, et faisant claquer comme un fouet
Le drapeau de bandes et d'étoiles aux trois couleurs...

Sounds of the ship: voices in a passageway.
Creaking of woodwork, squeaking of hanging lamps,
Rhythm of machines, whiffs of their stale odor,
Cries eaten by the wind, jumbling the music
Of a mandolin picking "Sobre las olas del mar..."
And the usual drone that ends by being silence.

Oh! Up there on the bridge, the long fierce wind, the piratical wind
Whistling in the ropes and cracking the flag like a whip
Of stars and stripes in three colors...

MA MUSE

Je chante l'Europe, ses chemins de fer et ses théâtres
Et ses constellations de cités, et cependant
J'apporte dans mes vers les dépouilles d'un nouveau monde:
Des boucliers de peaux peints de couleurs violentes,
Des filles rouges, des canots de boix parfumés, des perroquets,
Des flèches empennées de vert, de bleu, de jaune,
Des colliers d'or vierge, des fruits étranges, des arcs sculptés,
Et tout ce qui suivait Colomb dans Barcelone.
Mes vers, vous possédez la force, ô mes vers d'or,
Et l'élan de la flore et de la faune tropicales,
Toute la majesté des montagnes natales,
Les cornes du bison, les ailes du condor!
La muse qui m'inspire est une dame créole,
Ou encore la captive ardente que le cavalier emporte
Attachée à la selle, jetée en travers de la croupe,
Pêle-mêle avec des étoffes précieuses, des vases d'or et des tapis,
Et tu es vaincu par ta proie, ô llanero!
Mes amis reconnaissent ma voix, ses intonations
Familières d'après dîner, dans mes poèmes.
(Il suffit de savoir mettre l'accent où il faut.)
Je suis agi par les lois invincibles du rythme,
Je ne les comprends pas moi-même: elles sont là.
O Diane, Apollon, grands dieux neurasthéniques
Et farouches, est-ce vous qui me dictez ces accents,
Ou n'est-ce qu'une illusion, quelque chose
De moi-même purement—un borborygme?

MY MUSE

I sing Europe, its railways and its theaters
And its constellations of cities, and yet
In my lines I bring the spoils of a new world:
Shields of hide painted violent colors,
Red girls, canoes of scented wood, parrots,
Arrows feathered with green, blue, and yellow,
Necklaces of virgin gold, strange fruit, carved bows,
And everything that followed Columbus into Barcelona.
My lines, you have the power, O my golden lines,
And the zest of tropical flora and fauna,
All the majesty of my native mountains,
Buffalo horns, the condor's wings!
The muse that inspires me is a Creole lady,
Or the fiery captive the cavalier sweeps away
Lashed to his saddle, thrown across the rump,
Helter-skelter with precious stuffs, gold urns, and rugs,
And you have been conquered by your prey, O *llanero*!
My friends recognize my voice, its familiar
After-dinner intonations, in my poems.
(Just put the emphases in the right places.)
I am set in motion by the invincible laws of rhythm,
I don't understand them myself: they're just there.
O Diana, Apollo, great neurasthenic
Savage gods, is it you who dictate these strains to me,
Or is this only an illusion, something
Purely mine—a borborygmus?

LE DON DE SOI-MÊME

Je m'offre à chacun comme sa récompense;
Je vous la donne même avant que vous l'ayez méritée.

Il y a quelque chose en moi,
Au fond de moi, au centre de moi,
Quelque chose d'infiniment aride
Comme le sommet des plus hautes montagnes;
Quelque chose de comparable au point mort de la rétine,
Et sans écho,
Et qui pourtant voit et entend;
Un être ayant une vie propre, et qui, cependant,
Vit toute ma vie, et écoute, impassible,
Tous les bavardages de ma conscience.

Un être fait de néant, si c'est possible,
Insensible à mes souffrances physiques,
Qui ne pleure pas quand je pleure,
Qui ne rit pas quand je ris,
Qui ne rougit pas quand je commets une action honteuse,
Et qui ne gémit pas quand mon coeur est blessé;
Qui se tient immobile et ne donne pas de conseils,
Mais semble dire éternellement:
«Je suis là, indifférent à tout.»

C'est peut-être du vide comme est le vide,
Mais si grand que le Bien et le Mal ensemble
Ne le remplissent pas.
La haine y meurt d'asphyxie,
Et le plus grand amour n'y pénètre jamais.

Prenez donc tout de moi: le sens de ces poèmes,
Non ce qu'on lit, mais ce qui paraît au travers malgré moi:
Prenez, prenez, vous n'avez rien.

THE GIFT OF ONESELF

I offer myself to each as his reward.
Here it is, even before you deserved it.

There is something in me,
In the deepest part of me, at the center of me,
Something infinitely barren
Like the tops of the highest mountains,
Something comparable to the blind spot in the retina,
And with no echo,
And yet which sees and hears,
A being with a life of its own, which nonetheless
Lives my whole life, and listens, impassive,
To all the chitchat of my consciousness.

A being made of nothing, if that's possible,
Insensitive to my physical suffering,
That doesn't weep when I weep,
That doesn't laugh when I laugh,
That doesn't blush when I do something shameful,
And that doesn't moan when my heart is aching,
That doesn't make a move and gives no advice,
But seems to say eternally:
"I'm here, indifferent to everything."

Maybe it is as empty as emptiness is,
But so big that Good and Evil together
Do not fill it.
Hatred dies of suffocation there
And the greatest love never penetrates it.

So take all of me: the meaning of these poems,
Not what can be read, but what comes through in spite of me:
Take, take, you have nothing.

Et où que j'aille, dans l'univers entier,
Je rencontre toujours,
Hors de moi comme en moi,
L'irremplissable Vide,
L'inconquérable Rien.

Wherever I go, in the whole world,
I always meet,
Around me as in me,
The unfillable Void,
The unconquerable Nothing.

CARPE DIEM...

Cueille ce triste jour d'hiver sur la mer grise,
D'un gris doux, la terre est bleue et le ciel bas
Semble tout à la fois désespéré et tendre;
Et vois la salle de la petite auberge
Si gaie et si bruyante en été, les dimanches,
Et où nous sommes seuls aujourd'hui, venus
De Naples, non pour voir Baïes et l'entrée des Enfers,
Mais pour nous souvenir mélancoliquement.

Cueille ce triste jour d'hiver sur la mer grise,
Mon amie, ô ma bonne amie, ma camarade!
Je crois qu'il est pareil au jour
Où Horace composa l'ode à Leuconoé.
C'était aussi l'hiver, alors, comme l'hiver
Qui maintenant brise sur les rochers adverses la mer
Tyrrhénienne, un jour où l'on voudrait
Écarter le souci et faire d'humbles besognes,
Être sage au milieu de la nature grave,
Et parler lentement en regardant la mer...

Cueille ce triste jour d'hiver sur la mer grise...
Te souviens-tu de Marienlyst? (Oh, sur quel rivage,
Et en quelle saison sommes-nous? je ne sais.)
On y va d'Elseneur, en été, sur des pelouses
Pâles: il y a le tombeau d'Hamlet et un hôtel
Éclairé à l'électricité, avec tout le confort moderne.
C'était l'été du Nord, lumineux, doux voilé.
Souviens-toi: on voyait la côte suédoise, en face,
Bleue, comme ce profil lointain de l'Italie.
Oh! aimes-tu ce jour autant que moi je l'aime?

Cueille ce triste jour d'hiver sur la mer grise...
Oh! que n'ai-je passé ma vie à Elseneur!

CARPE DIEM...

Gather this sad winter day on the gray sea,
A soft gray, the earth is blue and the overcast sky
Seems at once both hopeless and affectionate,
And see the room of the little inn
So gay and boisterous on summer Sundays,
Where we're alone today, come
From Naples, not to see Baia and the Gate of Hell
But for our melancholy memories.

Gather this sad winter day on the gray sea,
Dear friend, O my dear good friend, my companion!
I think today is like the day
When Horace composed the ode to Leuconoë.
It was winter then too, like the winter
Now smashing the Tyrrhenian Sea on opposing rocks,
A day when one would like
To thrust worries aside and do simple tasks,
Wise in the midst of a serious afternoon,
And speak slowly as we gaze out at the sea...

Gather this sad winter day on the gray sea...
Do you remember Marienlyst? (Oh, what shore
And what season are we in? I don't know.)
People go there from Elsinore, on pale lawns,
In summer. There's Hamlet's tomb and a hotel
With electricity, all the modern conveniences.
It was a Northern summer, luminous, gently veiled.
Remember: we saw the coast of Sweden across the way,
Blue, like this distant profile of Italy.
Oh, do you love this day as much as I do?

Gather this sad winter day on the gray sea...
Oh, to have spent my life at Elsinore!

Le petit port danois est tranquille, près de la gare,
Comme le port définitif des existences.
Vivre danoisement dans la douceur danoise
De cette ville où est un château avec des dômes en bronze
Vert-de-grisés; vivre dans l'innocence, oui,
De n'importe quelle petite ville, quelque part,
Où tout le monde serait pensif et silencieux,
Et où l'on attendrait paisiblement la mort.

Cueille ce triste jour d'hiver sur la mer grise,
Et laisse-moi cacher mes yeux dans tes mains fraîches;
J'ai besoin de douceur et de paix, ô ma soeur.
Sois mon jeune héros, ma Pallas protectrice,
Sois mon certain refuge et ma petite ville;
Ce soir, mi Socorro, je suis une humble femme
Qui ne sait plus qu'être inquiète et être aimée.

The little Danish port is peaceful, near the station,
Like the ultimate port of every life.
To live Danishly in the Danish sweetness
Of this town and its castle with domes of patinated
Bronze, to live in innocence, yes,
It doesn't matter in which little town, somewhere,
Where everyone would be thoughtful and silent,
Where one would wait for death in peace.

Gather this sad winter day on the gray sea,
And let me hide my eyes in your cool hands.
I need gentleness and peace, O my sister.
Be my young hero, my protective Pallas,
Be my sure shelter and my little town.
This evening, mi Socorro, I am a humble woman
Who knows only how to be restless and loved.

IMAGES

I

Un jour, à Kharkow, dans un quartier populaire
(O cette Russie méridionale, où toutes les femmes
Avec leur châle blanc sur la tête, ont des airs de Madone!),
Je vis une jeune femme revenir de la fontaine,
Portant, à la mode de là-bas, comme du temps d'Ovide,
Deux seaux suspendus aux extrémités d'un bois
En équilibre sur le cou et les épaules.
Et je vis un unfant en haillons s'approcher d'elle et lui parler.
Alors, inclinant aimablement son corps à droite,
Elle fit en sorte que le seau plein d'eau pure touchât le pavé
Au niveau des lèvres de l'enfant qui s'était mis à genoux pour boire.

II

Un matin, à Rotterdam, sur le quai des Boompjes
(C'était le 18 septembre 1900, vers huit heures),
J'observais deux jeunes filles qui se rendaient à leurs ateliers;
Et en face d'un des grands ponts de fer, elles se dirent au revoir,
Leurs routes n'étant pas les mêmes.
Elles s'embrassèrent tendrement; leur mains tremblantes
Voulaient et ne voulaient pas se séparer; leurs bouches
S'éloignaient douloureusement pour se rapprocher aussitôt
Tandis que leurs yeux fixes se contemplaient...
Ainsi elles se tinrent un long moment tout près l'une de l'autre,
Debout et immobiles au milieu des passants affairés,
Tandis que les remorqueurs grondaient sur le fleuve,
Et que des trains manoeuvraient en sifflant sur les ponts de fer.

IMAGES

I

One day, in Kharkov, in a part of town where working people live
(O this southern Russia, where all the women
With white shawls on their heads look like Madonnas!),
I saw a young woman returning from the fountain
Carrying, as they have since Ovid's time,
Two buckets hung from the ends of a pole
Balanced on her neck and shoulders.
And I saw a child in rags approach her and speak to her.
Then, tilting her body graciously to the right,
She made the bucket full of pure water touch the ground
On a level with the lips of the child who had gotten down on his knees
    to take a drink.

II

One morning, in Rotterdam, on Boompjes Quay
(It was September 18, 1900, about eight o'clock)
I was watching two young girls on their way to work,
And with one of the great iron bridges behind them they said goodbye,
Each to go her own way.
They hugged each other tenderly, their trembling hands
Wanted and didn't want to separate, their mouths
Withdrew sadly only to draw near again
As they stared steadily into each other's eyes...
A long time they stood that way very close to one another,
Straight and still at the heart of a bustling crowd,
While tugs wailed on the river
And whistling trains were shunted on the iron bridges.

III

Entre Cordoue et Séville
Est une petite station, où, sans raisons apparentes,
Le Sud-Express s'arrête toujours.
En vain le voyageur cherche des yeux un village
Au delà de cette petite gare endormie sous les eucalyptus.
Il ne voit que la campagne andalouse: verte et dorée.
Pourtant de l'autre côté de la voie, en face,
Il y a une hutte faite de branchages noircis et de terre.
Et au bruit du train une marmaille loqueteuse en sort.
La soeur aînée les précède, et s'avance tout près sur le quai,
Et, sans dire un mot, mais en souriant,
Elle danse pour avoir des sous.
Ses pieds dans la poussière paraissent noirs;
Son visage obscur et sale est sans beauté;
Elle danse, et par les larges trous de sa jupe couleur de cendre,
On voit, nues, s'agiter ses cuisses maigres,
Et rouler son petit ventre jaune;
Et chaque fois, pour cela, quelques messieurs ricanent,
Dans l'odeur des cigares, au wagon-restaurant...

POST-SCRIPTUM

O mon Dieu, ne sera-t-il jamais possible
Que je connaisse cette douce femme, là-bas, en Petite-Russie,
Et ces deux amies de Rotterdam,
Et la jeune mendiante d'Andalousie
Et que je me lie avec elles
D'une indissoluble amitié?
(Hélas, elles ne liront pas ces poèmes,
Elles ne sauront ni mon nom, ni la tendresse de mon coeur;
Et pourtant elles existent, elles vivent *maintenant.*)
Ne sera-t-il jamais possible que cette grande joie me soit donnée,
De les connaître?
Car je ne sais pourquoi, mon Dieu, il me semble qu'avec elles quatre,
Je pourrais conquérir un monde!

III

Between Cordova and Seville
Is a little station where, for no apparent reason,
The Southern Express always stops.
Vainly the traveler looks around for a village
Beyond this sleepy little station under the eucalyptus.
All he sees is the Andalusian landscape: green and golden.
But on the other side of the track, facing it,
Is a hut made of blackened branches and mud.
At the sound of the train some raggedy kids come out.
The older sister leads them, and comes up close on the platform,
And, without saying a word, but smiling,
She dances for pennies.
Her feet look black in the dust,
Her dark face is dirty and not beautiful,
And she dances, and through the big holes in her ashen skirt
You can see her skinny naked thighs moving,
And her little yellow stomach rolling,
And every time, a few gentlemen snicker
In the smell of their cigars, in the dining car...

POSTSCRIPT

O dear Lord, will it never be possible
For me to know that young woman out there in Little Russia,
And those two friends in Rotterdam,
And the little Andalusian beggar
And join with them
In an indissoluble friendship?
(Alas, they'll never read these poems,
They'll never know my name, or how tender my heart is,
And yet they exist, they're alive *right now*.)
Is it possible that the great joy of knowing them
Will never be granted me?
Because, I don't know why, Lord, it seems to me that with the four of them
I could conquer a world!

MADAME TUSSAUD'S

Il me semble que toute la sagesse du monde
Est dans les yeux de ces bonshommes en cire.
Je voudrais être enfermé là toute une nuit,
Une nuit d'hiver, par mégarde,
Surtout dans la sale des criminels,
Des bons criminels en cire,
Faces luisantes, yeux ternes, et corps—en quoi?
Mais, est-ce que ça leur ressemble vraiment?
Alors pourquoi les a-t-on enfermés, électrocutés ou pendus,
Pendant que leur image muette reste ici?
Avec des yeux qui ne peuvent pas dire les horreurs souffertes,
Mais qui rencontrent des yeux partout, sans fin, sans fin.
Les ferment-ils au moins la nuit?

MADAME TUSSAUD'S

It seems to me that all the world's wisdom
Is in the eyes of these wax figures.
I'd like to be locked in there all night long,
One winter night, by accident,
Especially in the criminals room,
Fine wax criminals,
Shiny faces, dull eyes, and bodies—of what?
But is this what they really looked like?
Then why were they locked up, electrocuted, or hanged,
While their mute images stand here?
With eyes unable to tell of horrors suffered,
But meeting eyes everywhere, endlessly, endlessly.
Do they close them at least at night?

156. CANNES.- Yachts dans le Port et la Californie - LL

LA MORT D'ATAHUALLPA

Pues el Atabalipa llorava y dezia
que no le matasen...
—Oviedo

O combien de fois j'ai pensé à ces larmes,
Ces larmes du suprême Inca de l'empire ignoré
Si longtemps, sur les hauts plateaux, au bords lointains
Du Pacifique—ces larmes, ces pauvres larmes
De ces gros yeux rouges suppliant Pizarre et Almagro.
J'y ai songé, tout enfant, lorsque je m'arrêtais
Longtemps, dans une galerie sombre, à Lima,
Devant ce tableau historique, officiel, terrifiant.
On y voit d'abord—belle étude de nu et d'expression—
Les femmes de l'Empereur américain, furieuses
De douleur, demandant qu'on les tue, et voici,
Entouré du clergé en surplis et des croix
Et des cierges allumés, non loin de Fray Vicente de Valverde,
Atahuallpa, couché sur l'appareil horrible
Et inexplicable du garrot, avec son torse brun
Nu, et son maigre visage vu de profil,
Tandis qu'à ses côtés les Conquistadores
Prient, fervents et farouches.
Cela fait partie de ces crimes étranges de l'Histoire.
Entouré de la majesté des Lois et des splendeurs de l'Église,
Si prodigieux d'angoissante horreur,
Qu'on ne peut pas croire qu'ils ne durent
Quelque part, au delà du monde visible, éternellement;
Et dans ce tableau même, peut-être, demeurent,
Toujours la même douleur, les mêmes prières, les mêmes larmes,
Pareilles au desseins mystérieux du Seigneur.
Et j'imagine volontiers, en cet instant
Où j'écris seul, abandonné des dieux et des hommes,

THE DEATH OF ATAHUALPA

Pues el Atabalipa llorava y dezia
que no le matasen...
—Oviedo

O how many times have I thought of those tears,
Those tears of the supreme Inca and his empire undiscovered
For so long, on the high plateaus, at the far shores
Of the Pacific—those tears, those poor tears
From those huge red eyes beseeching Pizarro and Almagro.
I thought about them, when I was a little child, standing
For a long time in a somber gallery in Lima
In front of that historic, official, terrifying painting.
There we first see—a fine study of the nude and of expression—
The wives of the American Emperor, mad
With grief, demanding to be put to death, and here,
Surrounded by clergy in surplice and crosses
And lighted tapers, not far from Fray Vicente de Valverde,
Atahualpa, lying on the horrible
And inexplicable device of the garrote, his brown torso
Naked, and his lean face shown in profile,
While at his sides the Conquistadors
Are praying, fervent and fierce.
This is one of those strange crimes of History.
Surrounded by the majesty of Law and the splendors of the Church,
So prodigious in their agonizing horror,
One cannot believe that they do not endure
Somewhere beyond the visible world eternally,
And that even in this painting, perhaps, always the same sorrow,
The same prayers, the same tears remain,
Like the mysterious designs of the Lord.
And I like to imagine, this very moment,
As I write alone, abandoned by gods and men,

Dans un appartement complet du Sonora Palace Hôtel
(Quartier de la Californie),
Oui, j'imagine que quelque part dans cet hôtel,
Dans une chambre éblouissante de lampes électriques,
Silencieusement cette même terrible scène,
—Cette scène de l'histoire nationale péruvienne
Qu'on serine aux enfants, là-bas, dans nos écoles,—
S'accomplit exactement
Comme, il y a quatre cents ans, à Caxamarca.

—Ah! que quelqu'un n'aille pas se tromper de porte!

In a suite of the Sonora Palace Hotel
(In the California quarter)
Yes, I imagine that somewhere in this hotel,
In a room blazing with electric lights,
This same terrible silent scene
—This scene from Peruvian national history
That we drum into our children in our schools back home—
Is happening exactly
As it did four hundred years ago at Cajamarca.

Ah, let's hope no one opens the wrong door!

TRAFALGAR SQUARE LA NUIT

Ne sens-tu pas, jeune mendiante, qu'il est beau,
Que c'est une chose précieuse, d'être là,
Errant dans ce désert architectural
Au milieu de la plus grande ville du monde, sous les astres
Perpendiculaires, astres malins, clignotants,
Réverbères embués de la cité céleste?
Ne songe plus à ta faim, mais joue
A deviner les lions couchés dans le brouillard bleu,
Au bord des terrasses d'eaux noires où stagnent
Les livides reflets des globes électriques...
Viens! je suis une fée, je t'aime, tout à l'heure
Tu auras un festin dressé pour toi seule et des fleurs dans ta
        voiture;
Viens seulement contempler encore quelques instants
La grande chose nocturne, plus belle
Que les déserts et que la mer, et que les fleuves des tropiques
Roulant dans la splendeur lunaire;
Oh, regarde en silence, te pressant contre moi,
Femme dédiée à la ville!

TRAFALGAR SQUARE AT NIGHT

Don't you feel it, beggar girl, how beautiful it is,
And what a precious thing it is to be here
Wandering in this architectural wasteland
In the middle of the greatest city in the world, beneath
The perpendicular stars, evil twinkling stars,
Cloudy streetlamps of the heavenly city?
Think no more of your hunger, but play
At guessing where the lions sleep in the blue fog
At the edge of terraces of black water where
The livid reflections of electric bulbs are stagnating...
Come with me! I am a genie, I love you, in a little while
You'll have a banquet spread for you alone and flowers in your
    carriage.
Just contemplate the great nighttime thing
A few moments more, lovelier
Than the deserts and the sea and the tropical rivers
Rolling in lunar splendor.
Oh, look on in silence, pressing yourself against me,
Woman given over to the city!

L'INNOMMABLE

Quand je serai mort, quand je serai de nos chers morts
(Au moins, me donnerez-vous votre souvenir, passants
Qui m'avez coudoyé si souvent dans vos rues?)
Restera-t-il dans ces poèmes quelques images
De tant de pays, de tant de regards, et de tous ces visages
Entrevus brusquement dans la foule mouvante?
J'ai marché parmi vous, me garant des voitures
Comme vous, et m'arrêtant comme vous aux devantures.
J'ai fait avec mes yeux des compliments aux Dames;
J'ai marché, joyeux, vers les plaisirs et vers la gloire,
Croyant dans mon cher coeur que c'était arrivé;
J'ai marché dans le troupeau avec délices,
Car nous sommes du troupeau, moi et mes aspirations.
Et si je suis un peu différent, hélas, de vous tous,
C'est parce que je vois,
Ici, au milieu de vous, comme une apparition divine,
Au-devant de laquelle je m'élance pour en être frôlé,
Honnie, méconnue, exilée,
Dix fois mystérieuse,
La Beauté Invisible.

THE UNNAMABLE

When I am dead, when I am one of our dear departed,
(At least will you remember me a little, people
Who rubbed elbows with me so often in your streets?)
Will a few images in these poems remain,
Images of so many countries, so many glances, of all those faces
Glimpsed suddenly in the moving crowd?
I've walked among you, dodging the traffic
Like you and pausing at shop windows like you.
I've complimented the Ladies with my eyes,
I've walked happily toward pleasure and glory,
Believing deep in my heart that it had happened.
I've walked along delightedly in the flock,
Because we're of the flock, me and my aspirations.
And if I'm a little different, alas, from the rest of you,
It's because I see
Here in your midst, like a divine apparition
That I rush toward to have it touch me lightly,
The spurned, neglected, banished,
Ten times mysterious
Invisible Beauty.

II

EUROPE

La douceur de l'Europe.
Étienne Pasquier

II

EUROPE

The sweetness of Europe
—Étienne Pasquier

Cunard White Star   'Lancastria'

A M. TOURNIER DE ZAMBLE

*en lui envoyant le manuscrit d'*Europe

Encore un poëme, cher Monsieur
Xavier-Maxence pour les dames;
Un poëme à la suite de ceux
Esquels je distillai mes âmes,
Car aussi bien j'en ai plusieurs.

De Pompier j'imite le style:
Cet auteur écrivait si bien!
C'était coulant, c'était facile:
Chacun y retrouvait du sien;
Je suis son disciple docile.

Mon éditeur, éditez-moi
Ce dernier effort de ma muse,
Le dernier (hélas) je le crois,
Car le génie à la fin s'use,
Et le cygne reste sans voix.

Trop de plaisirs et de mollesse
M'a l'esprit tout débilité;
L'hôtel où gîtent les bougresses
Plus que toi, Délos, j'ai hanté,
Et plus le bourdeau que Permesse!

TO MR. TOURNIER DE ZAMBLE

On sending him the manuscript of Europe

For the ladies, Xavier-Maxence,
Another poem by me,
Distillations of experience
In which you'll see
My several spirits are condensed.

Pompier's style I imitate.
That author wrote so well!
Supple facility incarnate.
In my literary cell
I am his novitiate.

Publisher, publish then
The final, alas,
The final effort of my pen.
The swan has sung his last,
My genius has worn thin.

Excessive pleasures and living too well
Have utterly weakened my soul.
I've haunted the hotel where fast ladies dwell
More than I have you, Delos,
And more than Permessus, the bordel!

I

Un minuit en mer comme il y en a tant:
Le Cunarder au bruit doux sur la mer sans lune.
Il ferait chaud, n'était ce vent.
Le bruit de la vague la plus voisine: un éclaboussement;
Et l'autre vague un peu plus loin: une aspersion;
Et l'autre encore: un grondement lointain;
Et l'autre, se retournant, fait «Chut!»
Et toutes les vagues de la mer longtemps murmurent.
Les salons sont pleins de lumière sous les ponts,
Et pleins de Messieurs en noir et de Dames en robes basses.
Savoure, ô faible coeur, l'angoisse de cette heure.
Ne songe plus qu'à ton enfance. Quoi, tu pleures?
Non, non, ne pleure pas: écoute les tziganes
Qui jouent dans la restauration, à l'arrière...
Le poète est debout auprès de sa compagne
Étendue sur un divan, sous des fourrures, à l'avant,
«Un ange, une jeune Espagnole» qui par instants,
Pensant à lui, lui dit à mi-voix:
«Mein Liebling!»
Et de nouveau le bruit indifférent des vagues.
Tiens, un éclair!
Mais non; ce n'est pas possible; il fait beau temps...
Et toujours le vent et le bruit des flots sans fin...
Encore un! Là, là-bas, regarde!
C'est toujours dans ce même coin du ciel.
Ça passe comme une faux sur des avoines.
Tiens, encore;
Ça dure une seconde à peine. On dirait
Que cela tourne.
Là: il passe!...
J'ai vu le feu retourner; le phare, comme un dément
Tourne sa tête flamboyante dans la nuit, géant derviche,
Et, dans son vertige de lumière,
Il éclaire la route de campagne, la haie en fleur, la chaumière,

A midnight at sea like so many others:
The Cunard liner moving softly over the moonless sea,
A cool breeze in the warm night.
The sound of the closest wave: a splashing,
And another a little further off: a spraying,
And another yet: a distant rumbling,
And another, rolling back, says, "Shush!"
And all the waves of the sea murmuring far out and away.
The lounges are lit up beneath the decks
All filled with Gentlemen in black and Ladies in low-cut gowns.
Savor, O faint heart, the anxiety of this moment.
Think only of your childhood. What? Are you crying?
No, no, don't cry: listen to the gypsies
Playing in the dining room aft...
The poet is standing near his lady friend
Draped along a divan, in furs, fore,
"An angel, a Spanish girl" who off and on,
Thinking of him, says in an undertone,
"Mein Liebling!"
And again the indifferent wash of the waves.
Look, lightning!
No, it can't be, the weather's too nice...
And always the wind and the sound of the endless waves...
Another one! Over there, look!
Always in that part of the sky,
Moving like a scythe through oats.
Another one.
Barely a second long. It seems
To be turning.
There: it's going by!...
I saw the light turning, the lighthouse, like a madman
Whirling its flaming head in the night, a giant dervish,
And in its dizziness of light
It flashes on the country road, the blooming hedgerow, the cottage,

Et le bicycliste attardé, et la voiture du médecin sur la lande,
Et les abîmes déserts où le paquebot fait route.
J'ai vu le feu tourner, et je me tais.
Demain matin, les gens du salon, montant sur le pont
Où le vent piquera leur joues et leurs yeux froids,
Crieront: «La Terre!»
Et s'extasieront dans leurs cache-nez.

Europe, c'est donc toi, je te surprends de nuit.
Je vous retrouve dans votre lit parfumé, ô mes amours!
J'ai vu la première et la plus avancée
De tes milliards de lumière.
Là, dans ce petit coin de terre, tout rongé
De l'Océan qui embrasse d'immenses îles
Dans les mille replis de ses gouffres inconnus,
Là, sont les nations civilisées,
Avec leurs capitales énormes, si lumineuses, la nuit,
Que même au-dessus des jardins leur ciel est rose.
Les banlieues se prolongent dans les prairies teigneuses,
Les réverbères éclairent les routes au delà des portes;
Les trains illuminés glissent dans les tranchées;
Les wagons-restaurants sont pleins de gens à table;
Les voitures, en rangs noirs, attendent
Que les gens sortent des théâtres, dont les façades
Se dressent toutes blanches sous la lumière électrique
Qui siffle dans les globes laiteux incandescents.
Les villes tachent la nuit comme des constellations:
Il y en a au sommet des montagnes,
A la source des fleuves, au milieu des plaines,
Et dans les eaux mêmes, où elles mirent leurs feux rouges...

«Demain, tous les magasins seront ouverts, ô mon âme...»

And the man late on his bicycle, and the doctor's carriage crossing the
    heath,
And the forsaken abyss the steamer glides over.
I saw the light turning and I fall silent.
Tomorrow morning the passengers will leave their cabins and go up on
    deck
Where, the wind stinging their cheeks and their cold eyes watering,
They will cry out, "Land!"
Ecstatic in their mufflers.

So it's you, Europe, you I surprise at night.
I find you once again in your perfumed beds, O my loves!
I saw the first and foremost
Of your billions of lights.
There, on that little spot of earth, eroded
By an Ocean that puts its arms around immense islands
In the thousand folds of its unexplored gulfs,
There are the civilized nations,
With their enormous capitals, so luminous that at night,
Even above the gardens, their skies are pink.
The outskirts stretch out into mangy flatlands,
Streetlamps light the roads beyond the city limits,
Shining trains slide through the underpasses,
The dining cars are filled with people dining,
Dark rows of carriages are waiting
For people to come out of theaters whose façades
Rise dazzling white in electric light
Hissing in milky incandescent globes.
The towns spatter the night like constellations:
There are some on mountain tops,
Where rivers begin, out on the plains,
And in the water, even, where their red lights are reflected...

"Tomorrow all the stores will be open, O my soul..."

II

Fi des pays coloniaux, qui n'ont pour eux
Que les merveilles de la nature, et n'ont pas su
Même se procurer un Théocrite.
Dégoût des jours passés sur le hamac,
En vêtements de toile, dans des villes sans boutiques:
Dégoût des chasses aux bêtes fauves, des résidences
Royales des Indes et des cités d'Australasie,
Où l'on ne fait que penser à toi, par toi, Europe.
Car là, dans le brouillard, sont les bibliothèques!
Oh! tout apprendre, oh! tout savoir, toutes les langues!
Avoir lu tous les livres et tous les commentaires;
Oh, le sanscrit, l'hébreu, le grec et le latin!
Pouvoir se reconnaître dans un texte quelconque
Qu'on voit pour la première fois! et dominer le monde,
Par la science, de la coulisse, comme on tiendrait
Dans un seul poing les ficelles de ces pantins multicolores.
Sentir qu'on est si haut qu'on est pris de vertige,
Comme si quelqu'un vous murmurait les mots:
«Je te donnerai tout cela», sur la montagne!

II

Fie on the colonies, which have
Only the marvels of nature, and didn't even know how
To get themselves a Theocritus.
Tired of days spent in the hammock,
Dressed in white linen, in towns with nowhere to buy anything,
Tired of going out hunting animals, tired of
The royal residences of the Indies and the cities of Australasia,
Where one does nothing but think of you, through you, Europe.
For there, in the mist, are the libraries!
Oh to learn everything! Oh to know everything! All the languages!
To have read all the books and all the commentaries.
Oh, Sanskrit, Hebrew, Greek, and Latin!
To find your way in any text whatsoever
Even at first sight! And to rule the world
Through knowledge, behind the scenes, as if you held
The strings of these colorful puppets in a single fist.
To feel so high up you get dizzy,
As if someone were murmuring to you,
"All this will I give to you," on the mountain top!

III

Europe! tu satisfais ces appétits sans bornes
De savoir, et les appétits de la chair,
Et ceux de l'estomac, et les appétits
Indicibles et plus qu'impériaux des Poètes,
Et tout l'orgueil de l'Enfer.
(Je me suis parfois demandé si tu n'étais pas une des marches, un
  canton adjacent de l'Enfer.)
O ma Muse, fille des grandes capitales! tu reconnais tes rythmes
Dans ces grondements incessants des rues interminables.
Viens, quittons nos habits du soir, et revêtons
Moi ce veston usé et toi cette robe de laine,
Et mêlons-nous au commun peuple que nous ignorons.
Allons danser au bal des étudiants et des grisettes,
Allons nous encanailler au café-concert!
Dis-toi
Que nous ne sommes ici que des hôtes de passage
Dont les empreintes marquent à peine, sans doute,
Sur cette boue légère et brillante que nous foulons.
Quand nous voudrons, nous rentrerons aux forêts vierges.
Le désert, la prairie, les Andes colossaux,
Le Nil blanc, Téhéran, Timor, les mers du Sud,
Et toute la surface planétaire sont à nous, quand nous voudrons!
Car si j'étais un de ceux-là qui vivent toujours ici
Travaillant du matin au soir dans des usines,
Et dans des bureaux, et allant dans des soirées,
Ou jouer pour la centième fois un rôle dans un théâtre,
Ou dans les cercles, ou dans les réunions hippiques,
Je n'y pourrais tenir! et tel qu'un paysan
Qui revient après avoir vendu sa récolte à la ville,
Je partirais,
Un bâton à la main, et j'irais, et j'irais,
Je marcherais sans m'arrêter vers l'Équateur!

III

Europe! You satisfy the infinite appetites
Of the mind, and those of the flesh
And of the stomach, and the unspeakable
And more than imperial appetites of Poets,
And all the pride of Hell.
(Sometimes I've wondered if you weren't one of those borderlands, a
   county adjacent to Hell.)
O my Muse, daughter of the great capitals! You recognize your
   rhythms
In the constant rumbling of these endless streets.
Come on, let's get out of our evening clothes,
Here's an old jacket for me and this wool dress for you:
Let's mix with the common people we don't know anything about.
Let's go down where the students dance, and to the dime-a-dance halls,
Slumming in night-spots!
Tell yourself
That we're just passing through,
Leaving shallow footprints
Disappearing in this shining mud.
For whenever we want we'll go back to the virgin forests,
The desert, the prairie, the colossal Andes,
The White Nile, Teheran, Timor, the South Seas,
The entire planetary surface ours for the asking!
Because if I were one of these people who stay in one place,
Working morning, noon, and night in a factory,
Or an office, going out evenings,
Or playing a part in a theater for the hundredth time,
Or in clubs, or at the races,
I couldn't stand it! And like a farmer
Who comes back after selling his crops in town,
I'd leave,
Walking-stick in hand, and I'd go, I'd go,
I'd walk straight toward the Equator without stopping!

Pour moi,
L'Europe est comme une seule grande ville
Pleine de provisions et de tous les plaisirs urbains,
Et le reste du monde
M'est la campagne ouverte où, sans chapeau,
Je cours contre le vent en poussant des cris sauvages!

For me
Europe is like one big town
Filled with goods and all the urban pleasures,
And the rest of the world
Is an open country where, hatless,
I rush into the wind with a wild wahoo!

IV

A Colombo ou à Nagasaki je lis les Baedekers
De l'Espagne et du Portugal ou de l'Autriche-Hongrie;
Et je contemple les plans de certaines villes de second rang,
Et leur description succincte, je la médite.
Les rues où j'ai habité sont marquées là,
Les hôtels où j'allais dîner, et les petits théâtres.
Ce sont des villes où ne vont jamais les touristes,
Et les choses n'y changent de place pas plus
Que les mots dans les pages d'un livre.

On quitte le «pueblo» un beau matin; on va
A la Estacion del Norte dans l'omnibus antique
De la Fonda de Aragon. Petite ville,
Reste tranquille, je te sais fidèle, je reviendrai:
Les Indes, le Japon, ce n'est pas loin pour moi;
L'année prochaine, ou dans quelques mois peut-être,
Passant à Barcelone ou à Séville, je prendrai
(J'aurai ce courage!) le Correo plein de lenteur,
Et l'omnibus de la Fonda de Aragon contiendra ce voyageur
Et le ballottera au rythme strident des vitres
Le long des rues étroites entre les maisons comme un décor,
Tout comme s'il était parti la veille et revenait
Après une visite à la ville voisine.

Et vous, ports de l'Istrie et de la Croatie,
Et rivages dalmates, vert et gris et blanc pur!
Pola dans la baie claire est pleine de navires
Cuirassés, entre des bancs de gazon vert, navires pavoisés
De gais drapeaux rouges et blancs sous un ciel tendre.
Kherso, Abbazzia, Fiume, Veglia, villes neuves,
Ou du moins qui paraissez neuves, sans qu'on sache
Pourquoi; Zara, Sebenico, Spalato, et Raguse
Comme un panier de fleurs incliné près des flots;
Et les Bouches de Cattaro, où l'on n'en finit plus

IV

In Colombo or Nagasaki I read the Baedekers
For Spain and Portugal or the Austro-Hungarian Empire,
And I study the maps of certain second-magnitude towns,
And I consider their succinct descriptions.
The streets I've lived on are marked there,
The hotels where I used to dine, and the small theaters.
These are the towns tourists never see
And things there never change place any more
Than words on the pages in a book.

One leaves the "pueblo" one fine morning, goes
To the Estación del Norte in the ancient
La Fonda de Aragon omnibus. Little town,
Rest easy. I know you are true and I'll come back.
The Indies, Japan, for me they aren't very far away.
Next year, or maybe in a few months,
Passing through Barcelona or Seville, I'll take
(I really will!) the Correo, slow as it is,
And the Fonda de Aragon omnibus will hold this traveler
And rattle him to the strident rhythm of windowpanes
Down narrow streets between houses like stage scenery,
As if he had left last night and is now returning
From a visit to the neighboring town.

And you, ports of Istria and Croatia
And the Dalmatian coast, green and gray and pure white!
The bright bay at Pola is full of warships
Between banks of green lawns, ships flying
Red and white flags beneath a delicate sky.
Kherso, Abbazzia, Fiume, Veglia, new towns
Or which at least seem new, who
Knows why! Zara, Sebenico, Spalato, and Ragusa,
Like a basket of flowers tilted near the waves,
And the Mouths of Cattaro, where you never

De suivre toujours la mer au milieu des montagnes
Crénelées d'inaccessibles citadelles vénitiennes.
O Cattaro, petite boîte, petite forteresse qu'on donnerait
Pour les étrennes à un enfant (il n'y manque pas même
Le poste des soldats verdâtres à la porte);
Petite boîte de construction, mais toute pleine
D'une odeur de rose venue on ne suit d'où.

Et, après ces pays en bois découpé et peint qui sent bon,
Et que d'austères et d'abruptes montagnes noires enveloppent d'ombre
    et de fraîcheur,
Aride, toi, ardue, route du Monténégro, route du vertige
D'où l'on voit les forts autrichiens et les vaisseaux, en bas,
Aussi petits qu'au petit bout de la lorgnette.
(O route! et chevaux monténégrins, quelles terreurs
Vous m'avez inspirées, dans ce vieux landau bleu!)
Le diligence rouge vole en avant
Dans ce pays de pierre grise, où un arbre
Est agréable à voir comme toute une forêt,
Dans ce pays gris et noir où, au fond des vallées
Profondes comme des puits, on aperçoit
D'invraisemblablement petits champs verts, bleus, jaunes et gris clair,
    encadrés de pierres,
Comme un lambeau du maillot d'Arlequin tombé là.
Mais Njégus est un village rouge et blanc, clair et gai,
Dans une vallée à peine sèche des eaux du déluge.
Routes tristes des environs de Cettigne (avec le Belvédere); et parfois
Dans la nette aridité grise de ses gouffres minéraux
Qui font penser aux paysages lunaires,
Éclate soudain, comme si les pierres parlaient, une musique
Dure, triste et bien scandée, et qui remplit
Le ciel encombré de rochers avec sa fanfare grandissante.
Et l'âme inquiétée se troublait et ne savait que répondre
A ces voix bien ordonnées entendues de toutes parts
Dans l'absolue solitude,

Stop following the sea even among mountains
Crenellated with inaccessible Venetian citadels.
O Cattaro, little box, little fortress one might give
To a child for Christmas (it even has greenish soldiers stationed at
    the gate),
Building blocks, but filled
With the scent of roses coming from who knows where.

And, after these countries of carved and painted wood that smells so
    good,
And which austere and abrupt dark mountains envelop in shadow
    and coolness,
You, dry steep road in Montenegro, road of dizziness
Where one sees Austrian forts and ships far below,
Small as if seen through the wrong end of opera glasses.
(O road and Montenegran horses! How
You terrified me in that old blue landau!)
The red coach shoots ahead
In this land of gray stone, where a tree
Gives the pleasure of an entire forest,
In this gray and black land, where down in valleys
Deep as a well, one sees
Incredibly small fields, green, blue, yellow, and light gray, framed
    with rocks,
Like bits of Harlequin's tights fallen from the sky.
But Njegus is a red and white village, bright and cheerful,
In a valley barely dry from the Flood.
Sad roads around Cettigne (with its Belvedere), and sometimes
In the sharp gray dryness of its mineral pits
Reminiscent of lunar landscapes
There suddenly bursts forth, as if the stones were speaking,
A hard, sad, heavily accented music
That fills the rocky sky with its growing fanfare,
And your anxious soul wavered and did not know how to answer
These regimented voices coming from everywhere
In the absolute solitude,

Quand paraissent enfin au détour d'une route les premiers rangs d'un
    régiment grenat et bleu.
Puis vers Rjéka, alors qu'on voit, comme dans un nouveau monde, le
    lac de Scutari,
Il y a de tristes boutiques en plein vent, tendues d'Andrinople rouge
    qui sent fort,
Et des Albanais blancs aux ganses noires passent farouchement,
Des pistolets à la ceinture...

Et tandis que les grands vaisseaux de l'Orient et du Pacifique
Dorment sous la parure de tous leurs feux allumés,
Dans l'immense port d'Extrême-Orient, je revois
De la fenêtre de la salle à manger du Grand Hôtel, à Cettigne,
Les maisons basses et peintes en couleurs ternes,
Et la tristesse des villes slaves, plus triste
D'être dépaysée dans ce pays.
L'énorme chien du Grand-Hôtel Vuletich—*Turc,* je crois—il me semble
Le revoir couché au soleil, bonne bête couleur de café au lait;
Il dormait dans le calme du hameau-capitale...
Pauvre gros Turc, peut-être il est crevé, à présent...

When finally the first rows of a blue and garnet regiment appear at a
   bend in the road.
Then toward Rijeka and you see, all at once, as if in a new world,
   Lake Scutari,
There are open-air markets, covered with Turkey red cotton with its
   strong smell,
And white Albanians with black braids storm past,
Pistols in their belts...

And while the big steamers from the Orient and the Pacific
Sleep under the tiara of all their lights
In the immense Far Eastern port, I see again,
From a window in the dining room of the Grand Hotel at Cettigne,
The squat houses in their drab colors,
And the sadness of Slavic towns,
Sadder even than being a stranger here.
The huge dog at the Grand Hotel Vuletich—*Turk,* I think his name
   was—I seem
To see him again, asleep in the sun, a nice doggy the color of coffee
   with cream,
Sleeping in the quiet of this hamlet-capital...
Poor big Turk, maybe dead now...

V

Eau de l'Océan Atlantique
Dans la baignoire d'argent de ma maison de Londres,
Que ton odeur m'est douce et âpre, tandis
Que d'un bras humide
J'agite devant ma face un éventail parfumé!
Oh! ici enfin je suis bien, avec l'Océan chez moi
Et Grosvenor Square vu à travers mille fleurs aux fenêtres.
Ma belle maison! (Combien différente
De celle où je naquis à Campamento,
Au bord du désert d'Arequipa—au diable.)
Mais quoi! je sens qu'il faut à ce coeur de vagabond
La trépidation des trains et des navires,
Et une angoisse sans bonheur sans cesse alimentée.

V

Atlantic Ocean water
In the silver bathtub of my London house,
How bittersweet you smell, as I,
With a damp arm,
Wave a perfumed fan before my face!
Oh! It's so wonderful here at last, with the Ocean in my house
And Grosvenor Square seen through a thousand flowers at the
    windows.
My beautiful house! (How different
From the one where I was born at Campamento,
On the edge of the Arequipa Desert—in the middle of nowhere.)
But what! I feel this vagabond heart can't live without
The trembling of trains and ships
And an unhappy anguish forever fed.

VI

Fillettes qui vendez les journaux, court-vêtues,
En bleu clair avec des cols marins blancs,
Vous revoilà, toujours pour moi mystérieuses.
On ne sait: vous avez entre douze et vingt ans;
On se demande si vous avez des amoureux;
Vous vous ressemblez non seulement de costume,
Mais de visage, beaux visages blancs, brillants,
Aux traits aimablement durs, aux yeux farouches et bleus.
Il y a quelques années, je fus amoureux de vous toutes,
Comme j'ai été amoureux des bouquetières romaines,
Des jeunes filles de l'île de Marken, qu'on va voir d'Amsterdam,
Des paysannes de Corfou, et même aussi
D'une fausse bohémienne joueuse d'orgue de Barbarie à Londres.
Le déguisement émeut toujours mon coeur de poète,
Et votre vue me fait imaginer des aventures.

Djürgarden, jardins pâles loin des longs quais de pierres
Grises d'un gris si doux, si pur et estival!
Je veux errer dans ces bocages, le long de ces théâtres,
Le coeur tout alourdi de caloric-punch glacé.
J'irai dans les jardins des restaurations
Où des messieurs enivrés dorment sur les tables;
J'irai entendre là les derniers airs de Berlin.
Et puis je regarderai l'étalage merveilleux
Du marchand de phonographes qui est au coin de l'Arsenalsgatan
Et la statue de Charles XII me sourira dans les verdures de cette place
    ombreuse et douce
Où j'ai souffert.

VI

STOCKHOLM

You little girls selling newspapers in light
Blue short skirts with white middy tops,
There you are again, always mysterious to me,
Somewhere between twelve and twenty.
One wonders if you have lovers.
You all look alike not only in the way you dress
But in your faces, beautiful white shining faces
With amiably hard features and wild blue eyes.
A few years ago I was in love with all of you,
The way I'd fallen in love with Roman flower girls,
The young girls on the island of Marken—that one goes to see from
    Amsterdam—
The country girls of Corfu, and even
A phony bohemian organ-grinder in London.
Disguise always touches my poetic heart
And the sight of you arouses my imagination.

Djürgarden, with pale gardens far from the long stone embankments,
Stones of a gray so soft, so pure, so summery!
I want to wander through these groves, past these theaters,
My heart heavy with iced caloric punch.
I'll go to garden restaurants
Where drunken gentlemen sleep on the tables.
There I'll hear the latest tunes from Berlin.
And then I'll see the marvelous display
In the window of the phonograph dealer at the corner of
    Arsenalsgatan
And the statue of Charles XII will smile down at me in the greenery of
    that sweet and shady square
Where I have suffered.

Stromparterren, place où l'on boit, au bord des eaux,
Comme dans l'eau, et sous un pont, sous des feuillages,
Le soir, du caloric-punch, et des liqueurs que l'on ne sert,
Qu'en flacons d'un quart de litre, qu'il faut bien vider!
Cela est la plus douce chose de Stockholm.
Cela fait penser à Venise et à des soirs sur la Tamise,
Et c'est plus beau que les marchandes de journaux...
Et, pour vous garantir de l'humidité des soirs,
On vous fait envelopper d'une couverture de laine
D'un rouge éclatant, en sorte
Que les dames sont toutes des petits Chaperons-Rouges.

1905.

Stromparterren, square where people drink, at the water's edge,
As if in the water, and under a bridge, with leaves overhead,
In the evening, caloric punch, and liquors served
Only in half-pint decanters, and you have to drink it all!
That's the sweetest thing in Stockholm.
It makes one think of Venice and evenings on the Thames,
Even more beautiful than the newsgirls...
And to protect you from the evening damp
They wrap you in woolen shawls,
Explosive red, so that
The women are all Little Red Riding Hoods.

1905

VII

LONDRES

Après avoir aimé des yeux dans Burlington Arcade,
Je redescends Piccadilly à pied, doucement.
O bouffées de printemps mêlées à des odeurs d'urine,
Entre les grilles du Green Park et la station des cabs,
Combien vous êtes émouvantes!

Puis, je suis Rotten Row, vers Kensington, plus calme,
Moins en poésie, moins sous le charme
De ces couleurs, de ces odeurs et de ce grondement de Londres.
(O Johnson, je comprends ton coeur, savant Docteur,
Ce coeur tout résonnant des bruits de la grand'ville:
L'horizon de Fleet Street suffisait à tes yeux.)

O jardins verts et bleus, brouillards blancs, voiles mauves!
Barrant l'eau de platine morne du Bassin,
Qui dort sous l'impalpable gaze d'une riche brume,
Le long sillage d'un oiseau d'eau couleur de rouille...

Il y a la Tamise, que Madame d'Aulnoy
Trouvait «un des plus beaux cours d'eau du monde».
Ses personnages historiques y naviguaient, l'été,
Au soir tombant, froissant le reflet blanc
Des premières étoiles;
Et les barges, tendues de soie, chargées de princes
Et de dames couchés sur les carreaux brodés,
Et Buckingham et les menines de la Reine,
S'avançaient doucement, comme un rêve, sur l'eau,
Ou comme notre coeur se bercerait longtemps
Aux beaux rythmes des vers royaux d'Albert Samain.
La rue luisante où tout se mire;
Le bus multicolore, le cab noir, la girl en rose
Et même un peu de soleil couchant, on dirait...

VII

LONDON

After falling in love with eyes in Burlington Arcade,
I slowly walk back down through Picadilly.
O whiffs of spring mixed with odors of urine
Between the gates of Green Park and the cab station,
How moving you are!

Then I'm on Rotten Row, toward Kensington, calmer,
Less poetic, less under the spell
Of these colors, these odors, and the rumbling of London.
(O Johnson, I understand your heart, learnèd Doctor,
That heart resonant with the noises of the big city:
The Fleet Street horizon was all you needed.)

O blue and green gardens, white mists, mauve veils!
Drawing a line across the dull platinum water of the Basin,
Which sleeps beneath the impalpable gauze of a thick fog,
The long wake of a rust-colored waterfowl...

There is the Thames, which Madame d'Aulnoy
Found "one of the loveliest waterways in the world."
Her historical characters would glide by, in summer,
With evening falling, crumpling the white reflections
Of the first stars,
And the barges draped with silk and princes floating
With ladies recumbent on embroidered pillows,
And Buckingham and the ladies-in-waiting to the Queen,
Moving softly forward, like a dream, upon the water,
Or as our hearts would be lulled along
By the lovely rhythms of the regal verse of Albert Samain.
The shining street with everything reflected,
The multicolored bus, the black cab, the girl in pink
And maybe a touch of sunset...

Les toits lavés, le square bleuâtre et tout fumant...
Les nuages de cuivre sali qui s'élèvent lentement...
Accalmie et tiédeur humide, et odeur de miel du tabac;
La dorure de ce livre
Devient plus claire à chaque instant: un essai de soleil sans doute.
(Trop tard, la nuit le prendra fatalement.)
Et voici qu'éclate l'orgue de Barbarie après l'averse.

The roofs wet with rain, the square bluish and all smoky...
The tarnished copper clouds slowly rising...
Everything suspended in a damp tepidness, and the scent of honey
    tobacco.
The gilt edge of this book
Grows brighter every second: the sun trying to come out, I guess.
(Too late: inevitably the night will overtake it.)
And now the barrel-organ bursts out after the sudden shower.

VIII

BERLIN

Jeune postérité du plus grand des grands hommes,
Tu débordes déjà sur le monde de tous côtés,
Et, depuis mon dernier séjour,
Moabit a grandi comme une ville américaine.
Mère aux nombreux enfants, Berolina féconde,
J'aspire ton air joyeux et froid, pur et grandiose
Avec délices, ce soir de novembre.
C'est donc l'air qu'il a respiré, lui aussi,
Le prince au nez proéminent hors du tricorne!
On n'a rien changé aux vieux palais Louis-Quatorze. Ici
Tout date du roi de Prusse, et rien d'important
N'a été bâti depuis 1810. Il reviendrait
A l'heure de la parade, un matin âpre et bleu,
Sur l'Opernhaus Platz, et retrouverait ·
A leur place éternelle, les vieux monuments pseudo-classiques;
Mais tout autour de lui,
Comme Boston, New York, San Francisco et Chicago,
Poussant vers les horizons leurs rues immenses et leurs maisons
    énormes
A n'en plus finir, sa ville!

VIII

BERLIN

Young descendents of the greatest of great men,
You are spilling over the entire world,
And, since my last visit,
Moabit has grown like an American city.
Mother to so many children, fertile Berolina,
I breathe in your air, so cold and blithe, pure and grandiose,
This delightful November evening.
It's the very air he breathed,
The prince with the nose that stuck out under his three-cornered hat!
The old Louis Quatorze palaces haven't changed a bit. Here
Everything dates from the King of Prussia, and nothing of importance
Has been built since 1810. He would come back
Some crisp blue morning, at the mounting of the guard
On the Opernhaus Platz, and he would find
The old pseudo-classical monuments in their eternal places.
But all around him,
Like Boston, New York, San Francisco, and Chicago
Pushing their immense streets and enormous houses toward the
    horizons,
With no end in sight, his city!

IX

Des villes, et encore des villes;
J'ai des souvenirs de villes comme on a des souvenirs d'amours:
A quoi bon en parler? Il m'arrive parfois,
La nuit, de rêver que je suis là, ou bien là,
Et au matin je m'éveille avec un désir de voyage.
Mon Dieu, faut-il mourir!
Il faudra suivre à travers la maladie et dans la mort
Ce corps que l'on n'avait connu que dans le péché et dans la joie;
O vitrines des magasins des grandes voies des capitales,
Un jour vous ne refléterez plus le visage de ce passant.
Tant de courses dans les paquebots, dans les trains de luxe,
Aboutiront donc un jour au trou du tombeau?
On mettra la bête vagabonde dans une boîte,
On fermera le couvercle, et tout sera dit.

Oh! qu'il me soit donné, encore une fois,
De revoir quelques endroits aimés, comme
La place du Pacifique, à Séville;
La Chiaja fraîche et pleine de monde;
Dans le jardin botanique de Naples
La fougère arborescente, l'arbre-jeune-fille
Que j'aime tant, et encore
L'ombre légère des poivriers de l'avenue de Képhissia;
La place du Vieux-Phalère, le port de Munychie, et encore
Les vignes de Lesbos et ses beaux oliviers
Où j'ai gravé mon nom de poète lyrique;
Et puis aussi
Cette plage, Khersonèse, près de Sébastopol,
Où la mer est parmi les ruines, et où un savant
Montre avec amour une affreuse idole kirghize,
Lippue, ayant un sourire idiot sur ses grosses joues de pierre.
Et surtout, ah surtout!
Kharkow,
Où je sentis, pour la première fois,

IX

Cities and more cities:
I remember cities the way one remembers love affairs:
Why talk about it? Sometimes, though,
At night, I dream I'm here or there,
And I wake up in the morning wanting to travel.
My God, death!
I'll have to follow this body through sickness and into death,
This body I had known only in sin and joy.
O store windows on big streets in the capitals,
One day you'll reflect this passing face no more.
So many trips in steamers and first-class trains,
Is an open grave the only thing they lead to?
They'll put the homeless stray in a box,
Shut the lid and that will be that.

Oh! Give me just one more chance
To see a few places that I love, like
Pacific Square in Seville,
La Chiaja cool and crowded,
The big tropical ferns in the Naples botanical garden
And the girl-tree I love so much, and also
The light shade of the pepper trees on Kephisia Avenue,
The square in Old Phalerum, the port of Munychia, and also
The vines of Lesbos and its fine olive trees
Where I carved my name as lyric poet.
And also
That beach, Chersonesus, near Sevastopol,
Where the sea runs up among the ruins, and where a scholar
Lovingly points out a hideous Kirghiz idol
With a blubber-lipped idiot grin on his fat stone cheeks.
And above all, ah above all,
Kharkov!
Where I felt, for the first time,

Le soupir de vierge de la Muse soulever mon sein craintif;
Une ville pour moi:
Dômes d'or au sein des solitudes,
Palais dans le désert, chaud soleil rouge au loin sur la poussière;
Et, dans les quartiers pauvres,
Les mille enseignes des marchands de vêtements:
Les maisons basses, aux murs blancs couverts
De gros bonshommes peints, sans tête...

The virgin sigh of the Muse lift up my timid heart.
My kind of town:
Gold domes in the heart of emptiness,
Palaces in the desert, hot red sun far away on the dust,
And in the poor neighborhoods
Thousands of signs for clothing shops:
The squat houses, their white walls
Painted with big fat men with no heads...

X

Et toi, Italie, un jour, à genoux,
J'ai baisé pieusement la terre tiède, tu le sais;
O région du Ciel (n'es-tu pas de saphir, d'azur et d'argent?)
Région du Ciel, enchaînée
Au milieu des flots qui se font, pour l'exilée,
Pareils à un autre Ciel;
O enchaînée par les Néréides, comme Andromède,
En pensée, d'ici, encore une fois,
Je baise avec une horreur sacrée ton ventre
Et tes beaux flancs fécondés par les dieux...

X

And you, Italy, one day, on my knees,
I reverently kissed your warm earth. You know this.
O land of Heaven (are you not sapphire, silver, and azure?)
Land of Heaven, enchained
Among waves that become
Like another Heaven for her in exile.
O enchained by Nereids, like Andromeda,
In my thoughts, from here, once more,
And with a sacred horror, I kiss your belly
And lovely loins fecundated by the gods...

XI

Au bout de la petite rue en pente, je reconnais
Ce ciel et cette mer, et ce parfum aussi,
Et, rivage, je cours vers toi.
O mon Welschland béni! Romania solaire!
Glorieux fumiers, haillons divins, vous voilà;
Enfants nus, rouges vieillards fumeurs de pipes,
Vieillardes aux mains noires, adolescentes aux fortes voix,
Et toi, mer!
Laissez-moi seul, laissez-moi seul avec la mer!
Nous avons tant de choses à nous dire, n'est-ce pas?
Elle connaît mes voyages, mes aventures, mes espoirs;
C'est de cela qu'elle me parle en se brisant
Sur les cubes de granit et de ciment de la jetée;
C'est ma jeunesse qu'elle déclame en italien.

Un instant nous chantons et nous rions ensemble;
Mais déjà c'est l'histoire d'un autre qu'elle raconte.
Jetons du sable et des cailloux à l'oublieuse,
Et allons-nous-en!

XI

Down the hill where the little street ends, I recognize
That sea and that sky and that scent,
And, shore, I run toward you.
O my blessed Welschland! Sunny Romania!
Glorious manure, divine rags, there you are.
Naked children, ruddy old men smoking pipes,
Old ladies with grimy hands, teenage girls with loud voices,
And you, sea!
Leave me alone, alone with the sea!
We have so much to say to each other, don't we?
She knows my travels, my adventures, my hopes.
That's what she's saying as she breaks
On the granite and cement blocks along the jetty:
She holds forth in Italian on my youth.

One moment we're singing and laughing
But then she's telling someone else's story.
She's so forgetful:
Throw some sand and pebbles at her
And let's move on!

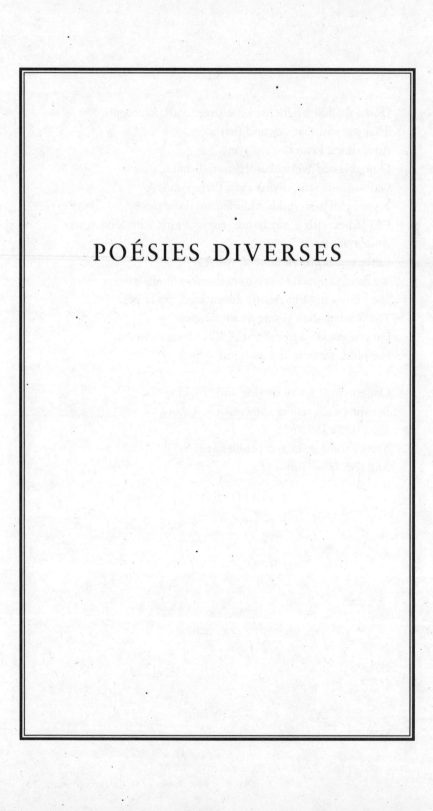

POÉSIES DIVERSES

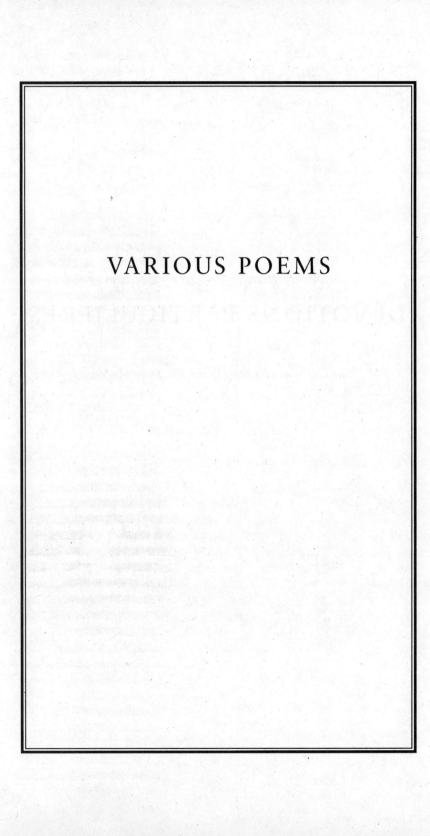

VARIOUS POEMS

I

DÉVOTIONS PARTICULIÈRES

Pour l'amie qui habitait la rue des Trois-Madones.

I

PRIVATE DEVOTIONS

For her who used to live on the rue des Trois-Madones

A M. VALERY LARBAUD

Tout ça, mon vieux Valerio, c'est très joli,
Surtout l'immobilité palpitante sous les longs passages de cieux,
Et ce voyage d'été à l'ombre de la fumée du navire...

Ou bien, ces matins de soleil et de janvier dans la salle du premier
    étage du casino,
Dans la ville en porcelaine avec son chemin de table de palmiers au
    bord de la mer bien réveillée,
Quand tu es seul et que tu sens gronder en toi
Le Français, comme un orgue et le tonnerre.

Mais n'y aurait-il pas moyen, avec moi, ton compagnon de tant
    d'années,
De sauter hors de ce temps, de cette fin du Moyen Age, de ces pauvres
    dernières modes de Paris-Londres-Vienne,
Dans le soleil et l'air tiède de l'Empire?

Comme ces poissons rouges de Valbois, par les journées chaudes,
Hors de ce que cet homme, chez ta mère, appelait:
l'*Arauquarium?*

                                    —A. O. BARNABOOTH.

TO MR. VALERY LARBAUD

All that, my old Valerio, that's all well and good,
Above all the palpitating immobility beneath long stretches of sky,
And that summer voyage in the shadow of smoke from the ship...

Or those mornings of sun and January in the hall on the second floor
    of the casino,
In that porcelain city with its border of palmtrees embroidered along
    the sparkling sea,
When you're alone and you feel
French rumbling inside you like an organ and thunder.

But wouldn't there be a way, with me, your companion of so many
    years,
To leap out of this era, this end of the Middle Ages, these miserable
    latest Paris-London-Vienna fashions,
Into the sun and warm air of the Empire?

Like those goldfish at Valbois during a hot spell,
Out of what that man at your mother's called
The *Arauquarium*?

—A. O. BARNABOOTH

DE L'IMPÉRIALE

Hymne

Les boulevards de brume rose,
Les ombres du soir vert et bleu,
Tous ces gens et toutes ces choses,
Tout cela, c'est à vous, mon Dieu.

Le sourd grondement de la ville,
Ne résonne qu'en votre honneur;
Et nous, d'un coeur simple et docile,
Nous vous louons sur la hauteur.

La tâche du jour est finie:
Nous rentrons fatigués chez nous,
Mais le meilleur de notre vie,
Seigneur: notre joie, est à vous!

FROM THE DOUBLE-DECKER BUS

Hymn

The boulevards of pink mist
The evening shadows green and blue
All these people and all these things
Belong, O Lord, to you.

The dull city rumble
Echoes to your sky.
With hearts meek and humble
We praise you upon high.

Tired we go back home.
The daily task is through.
But the best part of our life,
Lord, our joy, belongs to you.

WESTON-SUPER-MARE

MIDI

La pluie tombera tout le jour
Sur les terrasses qui se dressent
Entre le ciel en mouvement
Et les régions solennelles
De l'Empire du Soleil Blanc.

La Montagne-Inconnue se voile,
Et les gardiens de l'estuaire,
Les deux éléphants échoués,
Plongent dans l'immense brouillard
Et partent pour l'île d'argent.

Mais dans le jardin triste et bleu
Méditant sur ce midi sombre,
Où les capucines froissées
S'affalent et mêlent, pressées,
Leur robe jaune-orange et rouge;

On découvre, au bout d'un moment,
Quand on se croyait le plus seul,
Le nid, sous le porche abrité,
Où beaucoup d'yeux clairs et tranquilles
Regardent le jardin fumer.

Oh! comme la pluie les rend sages,
Et comme elles se taisent bien!
Et comme elles sont attentives
A tous ces regards blancs qui bougent
Dans les buis et les lauriers noirs!

WESTON-SUPER-MARE

NOON

The rain will fall all day
On terraces that rise
Between the moving sky
And the solemn regions
Of the Empire of the White Sun.

The Unknown Mountain veils itself,
And the guardians of the estuary,
The two stranded elephants,
Plunge into the immense mist
And depart for the silver isle.

But in the sad blue garden
Musing on this gloomy noon,
Where ruffled nasturtiums
Droop and intermingle, pressed close,
Their orange-yellow and red dresses,

You discover, after a moment,
When you thought yourself most alone,
The nest, under the screened porch,
Where many calm, clear eyes
Watch the steaming garden.

Oh! how the rain makes them good,
And how nice and quiet they are!
And how they pay attention
To those white glances stirring
In the box trees and black laurels!

Est-ce bien là Maisie-la-Folle,
Et Gladys qui rit tout le temps;
Violette aux genoux écorchés,
Et Gwenny qui lance toujours
Son volant par-dessus le mur?

Is that really Crazy Maisie,
And Gladys who laughs all the time,
Violette with the skinned knees,
And Gwenny who always sends
Her shuttlecock flying over the wall?

MARSEILLE

S'il m'est donné de revoir Athènes, que mon navire
Sous la sainte Garde soit
De Celle qui préside aux routes de la mer;
Celle qui brille au-dessus des flots et du soleil;
La géante debout au fond des heures bleues;
La haute habitante d'or d'un long pays blanc;
Pallas chrétienne des Gaules.

MARSEILLE

If I am ever to see Athens again, may my ship
Under the holy Protection be
Of the One who rules over the seaways,
She who shines over the waves and the sunlight,
The giantess standing at the end of the blue hours,
The tall golden inhabitant of a long white land,
Christian Pallas of the Gauls.

VALENCE-DU-CID

Ay! Mare de Deu, yo no soc valencía!
Et tant de bijoux ruisselants, et ces deux Anges au bord de votre
    manteau
Et à votre bras ce bâton de commandement, ce cep centurionique,
Ceinturé et couronné d'or, offert par un Roi d'Espagne,—
Tout cela intimide
Le plus couard de Vos soldats,
O plus justement que Faustine
Mater Castrorum appelée!
Et comment remercierai-je cette belle Brigadière-Générale,
Sinon en langue impériale?
Aixina:
«Ave...»
Comme je le fis jadis agenouillé devant le piédestal,
Mientras todos alrededor, como el trueno, gridaban:
«Magna Diana Ephesiorum!»
Y cuando Filius Tuus obumbravit super caput meum in die belli!

EL CID'S VALENCIA

Ay! Mare de Deu, yo no soc valencía!
And so many streaming jewels, and those two Angels at the hem of
   your cloak
And that scepter of authority on your arm, that centurionic staff,
Girdled and crowned with gold, offered by a King of Spain—
All of it intimidates
The most cowardly of Your soldiers,
O more justly than Faustina
Named Mater Castrorum!
And how shall I thank that beautiful lady Brigadier-General,
If not in the imperial tongue?
Aixina:
"Ave..."
As I once did, kneeling before your pedestal,
Mientras todos alrededor, como el trueno, gridaban:
"Magna Diana Ephesiorum!"
Y cuando Filius Tuus obumbravit super caput meum in die belli!

MILAN

Madonnina gentile
J'ai mis sous Votre protection mon amour.
Sous votre manteau qu'il repose, et dans votre ombre comme
Votre Poète, Comante Eginetico, dans une église de Parme,
Sous Votre image, qui est une poupée chargée de bijoux dans un
   berceau de cristal.
Maria bambina santissima,
Maria santissima, bambina,
Ah! dans mon coeur fais settina,
Sur mon coeur, comme lorsqu'aux rives d'Écosse et d'Angleterre
Je portais Votre image, avec les noms d'Ambroise et de Milan, dans un
   scapulaire.
Et mon Ange gardien
When he looks into it,
He will find in it
Just a Tiny Girl.

MILAN

Madonnina gentile
I've placed my love in your safekeeping.
May it rest beneath Your mantle, and in Your shadow, like
Your Poet, Comante Eginetico, in a church in Parma,
Under Your image, which is a doll covered with jewels in a crystal
    cradle.
Maria bambina santissima,
Maria santissima, bambina,
Ah! make a settina in my heart,
On my heart, as when I carried Your image to the shores of Scotland
    and England,
With the names of Ambrose and Milan, in a scapular.
And my guardian Angel
When he looks into it
He will find in it
Just a Tiny Girl.

II

LA NEIGE

II

SNOW

LA NEIGE

Chansos, vos poguetz ir por tot lo mon...

Un año más und iam eccoti mit uns again
Pauvre et petit on the graves dos nossos amados édredon
E pure piously tapándolos in their sleep
Dal pallio glorios das virgens und infants.
With the mind's eye ti seguo sobre Ievropa estesa,
On the vast Northern pianure dormida, nitida nix,
Oder on lone Karpathian slopes donde, zapada,
Nigrorum brazilor albo di sposa velo bist du.
Doch in loco nullo more te colunt els meus pensaments
Quam in Esquilino Monte, ove della nostra Roma
Corona de plata eres,
Dum alta iaces on the fields so dass kein Weg se ve
Y el alma, d'ici détachée, su camin finds no cêo.

Bergen-op-Zoom, 29.XII.1934.

LA NEIGE

(Réduction au français par Valery Larbaud)

Encore une année et te revoici déjà parmi nous,
Pauvre et petit, sur les tombes de nos aimés, édredon,
Et pourtant les recouvrant pieusement dans leur sommeil
Du pallium glorieux des vierges et des enfants.
Des yeux de la pensée je te suis sur l'Europe étendue,
Ou sur les pentes solitaires des Carpathes, où tu es, neige,
Des noirs sapins blancs voile de mariée.
Mais en aucun lieu mes pensers ne te vénèrent plus
Que sur le Mont Esquilin où tu es de notre Rome Couronne d'argent,
Tandis que tu recouvres profondément les champs, cachant les routes,
Et que l'âme, d'ici détachée, trouve son chemin dans les cieux.

SNOW

My songs, you can go throughout the world...

Another year and you are already with us again,
Poor and small, on the graves of our loved ones, a quilt,
And yet covering them piously in their sleep
With the glorious pallium of virgins and children.
With the mind's eye I follow you stretched over Europe,
Or on lonely Carpathian slopes where, snow,
You are the white bridal veil of the dark firs.
But nowhere do my thoughts venerate you more
Than on the Esquiline where, of our Rome, you are the silver Crown,
As you place a deep cover on the fields again, hiding the roads,
And the soul, detached from here, finds its way into the skies.

Kajütenbureau H. G. Köhler
MÜNCHEN
Promenadeplatz 19   (Hotel Bayer. Hof)

NOTES

The page numbers below referring to Barnabooth's poems are those of the Pléiade edition, *Oeuvres de Valery Larbaud*. References to *The Diary of A. O. Barnabooth* are from the McPherson & Company edition. The reader should not confuse Barnabooth's *Diary* (*Journal intime*) and Larbaud's *Journal, 1912–1935*, which is not included in the Pléiade edition. The most easily available volume of the Barnabooth poems is Gallimard's Poésie series pocket edition, *Les Poésies de A. O. Barnabooth*.

PROLOGUE, 7

In an early version of his poem *Europe*, Barnabooth is amused to see himself, in fifty years, as the "head of the Borborygmists" (Pléiade, 1181).

1: *borborygmi*: The Latin medical term describing rumbling or gurgling noises in the intestines.

8: *this song of ourselves*: A reference to Walt Whitman's *Song of Myself*. Whitman was one of Larbaud/Barnabooth's chief poetic influences, particularly in the long, irregular line, the global perspective, and a love of the open road.

ODE, 11

This poem is "inspired by the author's trip to Russia in 1898 and by an actual incident on this trip, between Wirballen and Pskov" (Pléiade, 1194–95).

Barnabooth notes his travels across Germany "in the Harmonika-Zug" (*Diary*, 83). He also mentions that he once traveled across Bulgaria on the Orient Express but that he remembers only "vast melancholy fields of roses (with an even still more melancholy smell)" (*Diary*, 212).

10: *Harmonika-Zug*: A German express train, having a movable covered hangway with accordion walls between cars.

12: *Wirballen*: The German name of a town in SW Lithuania. Virbalis rail station, three miles to the NW, was an important customs station until 1945. *Pskov*: A Russian city SW of St. Petersburg.

16–17: *the beautiful soprano*: These lines recall Whitman's "The pure contralto sings in the organ loft" in *Leaves of Grass* (687) as well as his poem "To a Locomotive in Winter." There the locomotive is addressed as "Fierce-throated beauty!" and personified as an opera singer to whom Whitman addresses the "chant" of his "recitative" (482–83). Singing women also figure in Barnabooth's "Servants' Voices."

18: The Pléiade edition and the Gallimard Poésie edition both give "Et vous, grandes places" instead of the "glaces" of the 1908 edition and the *Oeuvres complètes*. We have corrected this error.

18: *Samnium*: A country in ancient central Italy, the modern Abruzzi and Molise compartimento and part of the Campani compartimento.

19: *Sea of Marmara*: The inland sea of the Mediterranean basin, between the European and Asiatic coasts of Turkey, and between the Aegean Sea and the Black Sea.

20: *South-Brenner-Bahn*: The railway that links Austria and Italy, through the Brenner Pass.

33: *vague things*: Reminiscent of Barnabooth's referring to his "boundless appetite for thousands of vague things: liberty, action, travelling" (*Diary*, 240).

CENTOMANI, 15

This poem, whose Italian title means "a hundred hands," reflects "the travel impressions of Larbaud in Basilicata, 1903" (Pléiade, 1195). In his *Diary*, Barnabooth mentions spending time in Basilicata (43). See also Larbaud's *Mon plus secret conseil* (Pléiade, 647–715) for an account of the unhappy love affair that occasioned this trip in southern Italy.

1: *Basento*: A river in Basilicata.

9: *Lago Nero*: No such lake appears on contemporary or modern maps of the region. Had Larbaud mistaken the tiny town (pop. c. 6,000) of Lagonegro, which *is* in the area, for "Lago Nero"? Near Lago Nero is a lake called Lago Laudemio.

11: *Lucania*: The classical name for Basilicata, a territorial division of southern Italy, described by the *Michelin Green Guide: Italy* as "indescribably wild" (171).

17: *Tito to Potenza*: A distance of no more than eight miles. Tito is SW of Potenza, in the heart of Basilicata. On the Instituto Geografico Militare map of Potenza-Bari for 1913, the tracks of the Naples-Taranto railway pass just to the north of Tito, hugging the Basento River all the way through Basilicata to the Gulf of Taranto.

NIGHT IN THE PORT, 19

This poem is "imaginarily situated in Tunis, which Valery Larbaud passed by in 1905, and whose port he never saw from the sea" (Pléiade, 1195). The eleventh edition of the *Encyclopedia Britannica* ("Tunis") gives the following description of the European Quarter, interesting in light of the poem: "From the landing stage a short street leads into the broad Avenue Jules Ferry or de la Marine running east to west and ending in the Place de la Résistance, on the north side of which is the Roman Catholic cathedral and on the south side the palace of the French resident-general, with a large garden... Electric trams run to the harbour and also in a circle round the native city... In the Avenue de France or Jules Ferry are the chief hotels and cafés, the casino-theatre, the principal banks and the finest shops... In the rue d'Italie...the post office" (Vol. XXVII, 392).

1: *Portugal*: Rather than referring to the country, this refers to the orange-scented cologne, Eau de Portugal.

33: *Jaba*: The name of Barnabooth's ship means "basket" (Cuban Spanish) or "crate" (American Spanish), as well as being the Spanish name of the Indonesian island, Java.

Also, during the War of 1812 the American commodore William Bainbridge (1774–1833) defeated the *H.M.S. Java* in a famous naval battle. Ironically, Bainbridge served against Algiers and Tunis in the war against the Barbary States, during which his ship ran aground on the Tunisian coast, whereupon he was captured and imprisoned for a time.

36: *dioramas*: In 1822 the pioneer photographer Louis Daguerre and his partner Bouton founded the Diorama, "a theater without actors, where extraordinary illusions were created with remarkable lighting effects and huge pictures shown on three separate stages. The audience paid 2 or 3 francs admission to be transported as if by magic to a Swiss valley, Canterbury Cathedral, the tomb of Napoleon at St. Helena, and other famous monuments and sights. The lighting effects made the pictures, which measured $45\frac{1}{2}$ by $71\frac{1}{2}$ feet, change as one looked at them. The viewer could hardly believe that he was looking at a painted canvas and not nature; the illusion of the paintings became even more astounding when coins thrown into what seemed to be deep space rebounded from the canvas and fell to the stage floor. In some of the later Dioramas the effect was of one image dissolving into another: an Alpine village was swept away by an avalanche; darkness filled a church, candles were lighted, the faithful came to Midnight Mass, then the dawn sun lighted the stained glass windows" (Newhall, 2–3). Barnabooth is no doubt referring to a smaller, more portable "look-in" version of the Diorama.

THE MASK, 23

9: *some reader, my brother*: This phrasing is reminiscent of Charles Baudelaire's poem "Au lecteur" ("To the Reader"), which addresses a "hypocrite lecteur,—mon semblable,—mon frère" ("hypocritical reader—my double—my brother").

INDIAN OCEAN, 25

The opening lines of this poem recall a lovely entry, dated 18 July 1912, in Larbaud's *Journal*: "This evening to the *cinematografo*, not long (the smell too strong). Then along the lake. From the Campo di Marte—it had rained about half past five or six o'clock—nothing visible but the lights. So that there seemed to be *something new* in the sky: a slightly slanting line of big stars going up to mix in a shining array of fifty other bright big stars. And along the first line of stars, two luminous bodies creeping slowly, one up the other down. —Of course: the *funicolare* and Brunate on the top of the mountain over Como. Sometimes long and large flashes of lightning lighted everything and showed the boundaries between the mountains and the sky. Otherwise, there was no outline visible: all the same gray-blue mist" (25).

3: *Crucero*: The Southern Cross constellation (Spanish).

5: *Dutch East Indies*: The insular part of Southeast Asia, comprised of Indonesia and the Philippines.

17–20: A morning that Larbaud was later to describe as "one of the most beautiful of [my] youth" (Delvaille, 26).

18: *rue de Noailles*: An extension of the rue Cannebière, both streets being the center of life in Marseille.

20: *Vieux Port*: The old port of Marseille, forming a kind of appendix to the current port.

20: *Château d'If*: A castle built in 1524 by Francis I, long used as a state prison, and made famous by Alexandre Dumas' novel *The Count of Monte Cristo*. If is a rocky islet off the coast of Marseille.

NEVERMORE..., 27

The earlier title of this poem was "'Song of the Soul.' This piece was inspired by a sojourn of several days on the banks of Lake Starnberg in Bavaria in 1902, and [Larbaud's] impressions of a trip to Ragusa and Montenegro in 1903" (Pléiade, 1195). The sadness, despondency, and terror expressed in some of Barnabooth's poems burst into his *Diary* and into Larbaud's own *Journal* (wherein he is assailed by "The Mood"). The title, given in English by Barnabooth, doubtless refers to Poe's poem, "The Raven." Paul Verlaine (1844–1896) and Jean Moréas (1856–1910) also wrote poems with the English title "Nevermore."

15: *bay of Gravosa*: Gravosa (the Italian name for Gruz) is the commercial port of Dubrovnik (in Italian, Ragusa), in the Adriatic.

L'ETERNA VOLUTTA, 31

In his *Diary*, Barnabooth writes: "But my disgust with myself is none the less sincere and I feel that it is justified. When I examine myself closely I find myself really vile and stupid, and base... It was at the time when I had begun to discover my faults, though, being dominated by my vanity, I was fain to turn them into qualities and gloried in my baseness (in the moment of absolute despair when I composed a poem entitled *L'Eterna Voluttà*)" (58). The title was taken from a poem published in a Naples newspaper in 1903, part of which reads:

> Canta la fé, l'amore,
> L'eterna voluttà,
> Canta finch'il tuo cuore
> Un sol palpito avrà.

> *(Sing of faith, love,*
> *Eternal desire,*
> *Sing until your heart*
> *Has just one beat left.)*

(Pléiade, 1199)

18: *colorada*: "Red" or "reddish," in Spanish; here an adjective used with substantive force: red woman.

25: *the Danieli*: One of the major hotels in Venice.

35: *when not ill*: The wind, on this trip, caused Larbaud to contract conjunctivitis.

39: *Boreas*: The Latin name of the North Wind.

46: *Bonifacio*: A town on the southernmost tip of Corsica, on the Strait of Bonifacio, which separates Corsica from Sardinia.

47: *Messina's Faro*: Messina is a Sicilian port city seven miles SW of the promontory fortress of Faro ("lighthouse" in Italian). The Straits of Messina separate Sicily from the Italian mainland. *Scylla*: This is the area of the monsters Scylla and Charybdis, who decimate Odysseus' crew (*Odyssey*, Book XII). The monsters were legendarily located in the Straits of Messina and were feared by sailors in antiquity. The unpredictable currents do, in fact, present difficulties for seacraft, especially in a strong wind.

49: *The Lipari*: A group of small volcanic islands near the toe of the Italian boot. They are: Lipari (which lends its name to the entire archipelago), Stromboli, Salina, Filicudi, Alicudi, Vulcano, and Panarea. The island of Aiolie, the home of Aeolus, the lord of the winds, has generally been identified with one of this group, and they are also known as the Aeolean Islands. The "few lights" in this poem suggest those of Stromboli, an active volcano. Vulcano contains a still smoking crater that erupted in 1888–89, causing considerable damage.

THE OLD STATION AT CAHORS, 37

There is an undercurrent of sexuality in this poem, the train station seen in terms of an older woman whose sex life is only a memory. She is *désafectée* (put to another use; grown cold; like a soldier transferred because of a physical disability), *rangée* (set in her ways; no longer "on the loose"), *retirée des affaires* (retired from business; not in the running; has no sex life, after menopause). She is stretched out, useless, calm in the cool heart of her country, her waiting-room doors forever closed, with a cracked exterior. Her only visitor simply tickles her, in contrast to the past, when the back and forth (*ébranlement*: commotion, shaking, masturbation) of trains used to caress her. We mention this sexual imagery because of the interesting light it casts on lines 14–15, in which her double doors are open to "the charming immensity/Of the Earth, where God's joy must exist somewhere"—the word *joie* being slang for "prick," certainly "something surprising, dazzling."

Cahors is located approximately 350 miles south of Paris, on the railway line to Limoges.

SERVANTS' VOICES, 39

This poem "derives from various moments in the author's life in Valencia" (Pléiade, 1195). Barnabooth, in his *Diary*, mentions "old Lolita" and the female servants of the house (298), and is reminded of them by his friend Putouarey: "Do you remember your nurse when you were a child? You had negresses, over there, I suppose, a red Indian?" (170) And Barnabooth remembers that "a jolly little woman's voice sings out with a slight tremolo above the tremulous music" (203). This recalls the soprano in "Ode."

3: *jaula*: "Cage," in Spanish; this one for birds.

27: *"Paloma"*: "Dove," in Spanish.

27: *"Llora, pobre corazón"*: "Weep, poor heart," in Spanish.

29: *"Con una falda de percal blanca"*: "With a skirt of white percale," in Spanish.

30: *mornings on la Navé*: On November 22, 1905, Larbaud rented a small apartment at 34 calle de la Nave in Valencia (Aubry, 103).

31: *zarzuelas*: A type of song in Spanish musical comedies.

32: *"El arte de ser bonita"*: "The art of being (a) pretty (girl or woman)," in Spanish.

32: *"La gatita blanca"*: "The white kitten," in Spanish.

34: *"Anteayer vi a una señora"*: "The day before yesterday I saw a lady," in Spanish.

39: *Frizzy samba maids*: "Samba" is the feminine form of "sambo," meaning the offspring of Negro and Indian (or mulatto) parents. It is probably derived from the Spanish word *zambo*.

39: *red cholitas*: The diminutive of *chola*, meaning a Native American female of mixed ancestry, in Spanish.

48: *Because I loved you most for serious and sad*: In Larbaud's original the syntax in this line ("Car je t'aimais surtout pour douloureuse et grave") is Spanish, not French—a clever touch in this particular poem.

49: *sirandanes*: Riddles that come from Mauritius and surrounding islands. The first book about sirandanes, Charles Baissac's *Étude sur le patois créole mauricien,* appeared in 1880.

57: *Milordito*: A Spanglish word meaning "my little lord."

59: *criadas*: "Female servants," in Spanish.

NOVEMBER MORNING NEAR ABINGDON, 43

Abingdon is a small town six miles south of Oxford, on the Thames.

5: *Samain*: Albert Samain, French poet (1858–1900), the author of *Au jardin de l'infante, Aux flancs du vase,* and other collections.

ALMA PERDIDA, 47

The Spanish title means "lost soul." The last line is also found in Barnabooth's *Diary* (237).

8: *benzoin*: The use of tincture of benzoin in a hot, steamy bath suggests that Barnabooth suffers from pulmonary congestion (as Larbaud did). Perhaps it is the scent of benzoin on his fan in *Europe* V.5, in London, where respiratory disorders were more common than they are today.

11: *candies*: Perhaps the Spanish candies Barnabooth refers to in his *Diary* (305): "England is the country for kisses. They are what sweetmeats are in Spain."

13: *sweetness of being seated*: In his *Diary* Barnabooth ascribes this pleasure to his mother, who "profoundly enjoys the sensation of being seated" (234).

The title is "the name of a kind of song from the...Andes" (Pléiade, 1195). In his *Diary* Barnabooth notes a recurrence of the ennui that plagues him, "a disgust, an intolerable weariness," and relates it to the "'heavenly gift' of the poets...it really is a gift of Heaven, the gift of Apollo" (284), sentiments that are reflected in the last two lines of this poem. Barnabooth also notes, "In the fold of the water bobbed a green pumpkin" (103), similar to the flotsam in line 20 of the poem.

5: *Bosphorus*: The ancient Strait of Constantinople, connecting the sea of Marmara and the Black Sea. Istanbul is on its west bank.

9: *"Narrenschiff"*: Barnabooth's yacht takes its name from the satire *Das Narrenschiff* (*The Ship of Fools*) by Sebastian Brant (1457–1521).

10: *Euxine Sea*: The Greek name for the Black Sea, and perhaps the scene of the Argonauts' adventures.

16: *Ottoman Empire*: The empire founded by Osman (1288–1320), which lasted until 1919.

21: *Ausonia*: The name applied by Greek writers to Latium and Campania in Italy; the Augustan poets used it as a synonym for Italy.

22: *fiaschetto*: A small flask or bottle, in Italian.

23: *Tyrrhenian wave*: Synecdoche for the Tyrrhenian Sea, the part of the Mediterranean between the Italian peninsula, Corsica, Sardinia, and Sicily.

27: *Odessa*: A port city in Ukraine on the Black Sea. In 1905 a revolutionary focal point.

30: *"Ya que para mi no vives"*: "Since you no longer live for me," in Spanish.

38: *paseos*: "Streets," in Spanish.

40: *Little Cythera*: Probably the small Greek island in the Aegean Sea now known as Andikithera, near the larger island of Cythera (famous in antiquity for its temple of Aphrodite).

MERS-EL-KEBIR, 53

Mers-el-Kebir (Great Harbor) is an Algerian coastal town. This poem is "a remembrance of the author's trip to the Algerian port city of Oran in 1906, traces of which are found in 'Le Miroir du café Marchesi' in Larbaud's *Aux couleurs de Rome*" (Pléiade, 1195).

THE POET'S WISHES, 55

6: *Brompton Road, Marylebone, or Holborn*: Marylebone and Holborn are central London thoroughfares, as well as being city districts. Brompton Road is located directly south of Hyde Park.

12: *Vanity Fair*: In his *Diary* Barnabooth writes, "O little Vanity Fair, O charm of Europe" (Pléiade, 303). The term originated in Bunyan's *Pilgrim's Progress* (1678) and was used as the title of Thackeray's 1848 novel.

14: The decoration of graves on All Saints' Day is a custom dating to antiquity and signifies both remembrance and appeasement of the dead.

MUSIC AFTER READING, 57

13: *Serenos*: "Night watchmen," in Spanish. The *serenos* not only patrolled the streets, they also called out or sang the hours; hence the suggestion, in Larbaud's verb *psalmodieront*, of the singing or chanting of monks, perhaps at matins. (Decades after this poem was written the Spanish government modified the role of the *serenos*, commissioning them simply as municipal policemen.)

15: *St. Joseph's Day*: This important Feast Day is celebrated by the Roman Catholic Church on March 19. The third Wednesday after Easter is also the Feast of St. Joseph, who is the patron saint of the Church as a whole.

SCHEVENINGEN, OFF-SEASON, 61

"This poem dates from the author's trip to Holland in 1901" (Pléiade, 1195). Scheveningen is a fishing port in the Netherlands, on the North Sea, now a suburb of The Hague. Its development as a fashionable seaside resort dates from the nineteenth century. The first bathing establishment in Holland was opened there in 1818. This poem was written before Larbaud created Barnabooth.

THALASSA, 63

Thalassa ("the sea," in Greek) "reflects the impressions of the Adriatic sailed by the writer in 1903" (Pléiade, 1195).

10: *Corpus Poeticum Boreale*: Most likely Larbaud is referring to *Corpus Poeticum Boreale: The Poetry of the Old Northern Tongue from the Earliest Times to the Thirteenth Century*, edited, classified, and translated with introduction, excursus, and notes by Gudbrand Vigfusson, M.A., and F. York Powell, M.A. (London: Oxford at the Clarendon Press, 1883). Volume I: Eddic Poetry; Volume II: Court Poetry.

35: *"Sobre las olas del mar"*: "Over the waves of the sea," in Spanish.

MY MUSE, 67

"This work is one that most obviously bears the conscious influence of Walt Whitman" (Pléiade, 1195).

3–8: These lines refer to the triumphal return of Christopher Columbus to Barcelona, where at the royal court he exhibited the "rich and strange" spoils of the new-found lands.

12: *Buffalo horns, the condor's wings*: Tournier de Zamble's preface to the 1908 edition of these poems points out that this line (in the original Spanish "Los cuernos del Bisonte, las alas del Condor") is taken from the work of the Peruvian poet José Santos Chocano (1875–1934). Known as "The Singer of America," Chocano was one of the leaders of Latin American *modernismo*. He integrated indigenous themes in his books *Alma America* (*The Soul of America*, 1906) and *Primicias de Oro de Indias* (*First Fruits of Gold from the Indies*, 1934).

17: *llanero*: "Plainsman," in Spanish.

THE GIFT OF ONESELF, 69

Barnabooth tells us in his *Diary* that he wrote this poem (its title translated as "Gift of Self" by Cannan) in Florence, "opposite the cupola of San Frediano with its mournful windows" (118-119). The title appears also in the *Diary*: "Nobility comes entirely from the gift of oneself" (270).

CARPE DIEM..., 73

This poem, set on the Bay of Naples during winter, was written in Vichy in the summertime. This dislocation is slyly alluded to in the poem: "Oh, what shore / And what season are we in?"

In his *Diary* Barnabooth expresses the desire for anonymity found in the fourth stanza of the poem: "I abdicate my interesting personality" (234) and "Oh! to live as they do, on the philosophy of a health resort, the metaphysic of the Riviera!" (235).

7: *Baia and the Gate of Hell*: According to legend the port of Baia, on the Bay of Naples, was a rich Greek colony that took its name from Baios, the companion of Odysseus who died and was buried there. At the time of the Roman Empire it was a fashionable bathing-beach as well as a thermal spa with the most complete hydrotherapy facilities in the world. The Roman Emperors and patricians had immense villas and gardens there, all of which disappeared under the sea after a change in ground level. Baia is located in the Campi Flegri (Phlegean Fields). This landscape of dark, violent, inhuman beauty inspired Homer and Vergil, who based on it the myths of the Oracle (the Sybil at Cumae, nearby) and the Kingdom of the Infernal Regions. Lake Avernus is situated here. The ancients regarded it as the entrance to the world of the dead. From his poems, it seems probable that Horace visited Baia at least once.

12: *Horace... the ode to Leuconoë*: The title of Larbaud's poem is to be found in the last line of Horace's ode to Leuconoë (*Odes* I.*xi*):

> ...*carpe diem quam minimum credula postero.*
> (Seize the day, trusting as little as possible to the future.)

12: Barnabooth's visit to Baia reminds him of Horace's visit to the same locale. It is possible that the name Horace suggests Shakespeare's Horatio (Horace in French) and hence the Danish setting of *Hamlet*. Both Horace and Horatio are generous with advice. Barnabooth follows in this tradition.

13–14: These lines are translated from Horace's ode to Leuconoë:

> *seu plures hiemes, seu tribuit Iuppiter ultimam,*
> *que nunc oppositis debilitat pumicibus mare*
> *Tyrrhenum…*

> (Whether Jupiter has granted us many winters,
> or whether this is the last that now with its
> opposing rocks weakens the Tuscan sea)

Steele Commager, who provides the above literal version in his *Odes of Horace,* comments: "The striking word *debilitat*, 'lames' or 'enfeebles,' is better suited to a human than to a natural context, while the inversion that makes the winter cripple the sea with opposing rocks would be quite remarkable in a purely descriptive context" (Commager, 274). Larbaud has not quite caught the meaning of *debilitat* with his French *briser*, but, given his knowledge of Latin, was probably not intent on a literal translation.

20: *Marienlyst*: A Danish coastal resort just northwest of Elsinore.

44: *mi Socorro*: "My Succor," my aid, in Spanish. Two young Peruvian sisters figure in Barnabooth's *Diary*, Socorro and Conception Yarza, both of whom are his wards. Eventually he marries Conception.

IMAGES, 79

Charles Baudelaire's "À une mendiante rousse" ("To a Redhaired Beggar-woman") in *Les Fleurs du mal* (1857) is a precursor to part III of this poem.

I.1: *Kharkov*: The former capital of what is now the Ukrainian Republic.

I.5: Ovid's *Epistles from Pontus* (III.8) describes such a water-bearer.

II: This section and the last few lines of "Postscript" derive from a poem in Walt Whitman's "Calamus" section of the 1860 edition of *Leaves of Grass*. In "What Think You I Take My Pen in Hand?" Whitman says that he writes not to record pictures of greatness or glory,

> But merely of two simple men I saw to-day on the pier in the midst of the
>   crowd, parting the parting of dear friends,
> The one to remain hung on the other's neck and passionately kiss'd him,
> While the one to depart tightly prest the one to remain in his arms. (165)

III: Barnabooth's *Diary* (227–229) contains a sadistic scene involving the rich and the poor.

Postscript: 2: *Little Russia*: Former area with indefinite boundaries including Carpathian Ruthenia, eastern Poland, Ukraine, and the western shores of the Black Sea.

MADAME TUSSAUD'S, 83

The title refers to the London wax museum. Larbaud might have also had in mind the Pan-optikum, a wax museum he visited twice on a trip to Amsterdam in 1901. The Panoptikum featured a collection of famous murderers. Barnabooth's *Diary* refers to "the Panoptikeum [*sic*], where the characters of the Dreyfus affair, stuffed out in their faded uniforms, linger among the heads and hands cut off the most celebrated criminals in Denmark" (288–89).

THE DEATH OF ATAHUALPA, 87

The epigraph ("Then Atahualpa wept and asked that they not kill him") is from the Spanish historian Gonzalo Fernandez de Oviedo y Valdes (1478–1557). Not only had Oviedo seen Columbus previous to his first voyage to America, but he also visited America himself on several occasions in an official capacity. Appointed historiographer of the Indies, Oviedo wrote two historical works, *Sumario de la natural y general historia de las Indias* (1526) and *La historia natural y general de las Indias, Islas e tierra Firme del mar oceano* (1535–57).

2: *the supreme Inca*: Atahualpa (c. 1502–1533) was the last Inca king. After the swift triumph of a small band of invading conquistadors in 1532, "the emperor was brought to trial on as many charges as could be trumped up...convicted and sentenced to be burned alive that very night in the public square of Cajamarca... As the wood was about to be ignited, Atahualpa was told that his sentence could be changed to strangulation...if he would accept Christianity. He did, was baptized, and then garroted" (Mason, 136–137).

5: *Pizarro and Almagro*: Francisco de Pizarro (c. 1471–1541) and Diego de Almagro (c. 1470–1538), with a priest named Hernando de Luque, comprised the syndicate that initiated the conquest of Peru. Later disputes between Pizarro and Almagro plunged Spanish Peru into the first of a series of civil wars.

7: *a somber gallery in Lima*: When Francisco Contreras confronted Larbaud with the fact that the painting in question depicts the funeral rather than the execution of Atahualpa, Larbaud replied that it made no difference: "Barnabooth was so little then..." (Contreras, 17). The painting might well be *Los funerales de Atahualpa* by Luis Montero (1827–1869), a Peruvian artist trained in his homeland and Italy, where this painting was made in 1867. It depicts the grief-stricken wives of Atahualpa (though they are hardly naked) and the other elements described in the poem, though in the painting Atahualpa is already dead, laid out on his catafalque, with no garrote in sight. This affecting work was purchased by the Peruvian government, which used it for a while on the 500 Sol banknote.

13: *Fray Vicente de Valverde*: A Dominican priest who came to Peru with Pizarro after 1529. He conducted the crucial interview with Atahualpa in the great square in Cajamarca, surrounded by more than 3,000 of the Emperor's people, while Pizarro's artillery and troops, strategically placed in buildings and streets opening onto the square, looked on. Atahualpa listened through an interpreter to the priest's statement of the history and tenets of the Christian faith and the Roman Catholic policy. Fray Vicente then called upon the Inca to become a Christian and to acknowledge Charles V of Spain as his master. Atahualpa vehemently pointed out certain difficulties in the Christian religion, acknowledged the obvious greatness of the Spanish emperor, and then declined to accept either one. In fact he is said to have taken the Bible from the priest's hands and flung it resentfully to the ground. Pizarro gave his troops the signal for the attack. The Peruvians were cut down by the hundreds. When Atahualpa was later sentenced to death by fire, Pizarro's most influential advisors protested the decision, with Valverde being a notable exception.

15: *garrote*: A device used for the execution by strangulation of condemned criminals. The execution was performed by twisting a cord or bandage on the condemned man's neck until strangulation occurred, but later a mechanically operated metal collar was devised.

30: *the California Quarter*: The California Quarter is in Cannes (Pléiade, 1195).

TRAFALGAR SQUARE AT NIGHT, 91

In his *Diary*, Barnabooth writes: "Oh! If only it might happen once that a king married a shepherdess. King Cophetua married the beggar girl! Sometimes I feel inclined to go into the nearest hovel one morning and choose my wife and take her away, still sleeping, dead drunk, and bear her to the altar" (92).

EUROPE, 97

The epigraph is from Étienne Pasquier (1529–1615), French magistrate and author of *Recherches sur la France*.

TO MR. TOURNIER DE ZAMBLE, 99

Tournier de Zamble: Xavier-Maxence Tournier de Zamble, the fictitious author of the preface to the poems of the fictitious Barnabooth.

6: *Pompier*: Apparently another fictitious author, with his name derived from the French expression *le style pompier*, meaning a banal, pompous, and empty style.

19: *Delos*: The mythological birthplace of Apollo, Greek god of the arts.

10: *Permessus*: A river sacred to Apollo, which rose on Mount Helicon, the summit of which contained the sanctuary of the Muses.

I.2: *Cunard liner*: A transatlantic steamer of the Cunard Line.

I.19: *Mein Liebling*: "My love," in German.

II.3: *Theocritus*: Greek pastoral poet born in Syracuse c. 300 B.C.

II.7: *Australasia*: Australia and New Zealand.

II.19: *"All this will I give to you"*: A quotation from Luke 4:7, in which Christ is tempted on the mountain top by Satan. Barnabooth refers to the temptation in his *Diary*:

"I mean The World, what Satan called All This in the temptation: 'I will give you all this...'" (270).

III.20: *The White Nile*: That part of the upper Nile that begins in Lake Victoria. Near Khartoum it is joined by the Blue Nile.

III.20: *Teheran*: The capital of Iran.

III.20: *Timor*: An island in the East Indies.

IV.1: *Colombo*: The capital of Sri Lanka.

IV.11: *Baedekers*: Popular travel guidebooks in Barnabooth's time. They were published and sometimes written by Karl Baedeker.

IV.11: *Estación del Norte*: "North Station," in Spanish.

IV.17: *Correo*: "Mail coach" (or train), in Spanish.

IV.25: *Pola*: A sheltered bay in Croatia 40 miles SW of Fiume (Rijeka).

IV.28: *Kherso, Abbazzia, Fiume, Veglia*: Croatian ports and resorts, the last three here given their Italian and not their Croatian names (Opatija, Rijeka, and Krk).

IV.30: *Zara, Sebenico, Spalato, Ragusa*: Croatian towns on the Adriatic.

IV.32: *Mouths of Cattaro*: The Gulf of Kotor, a winding inlet on the Adriatic, touching on Montenegro and Dalmatia.

IV.36: *soldiers*: Larbaud/Barnabooth admired the beauty of regiments of real and (especially) toy soldiers. For instance, in his *Diary* Barnabooth writes: "And I remember a cavalry regiment: blue and red...neat and shining like lead soldiers taken out of the box for the first time" (213).

IV.53: *Njegus*: A mountain in Montenegro.

IV.55: *Cetinje*: Montenegran town near Lake Scutari.

IV.65: *Rijeka*: See note for IV.28 of this poem.

IV.65: *Lake Scutari*: Located on the border between Montenegro and Albania.

IV.75–77: Another dog named Turk that Barnabooth/Larbaud may be thinking of is the Newfoundland once owned by the family of Thomas De Quincey. The dog killed the young De Quincey's kitten, sending the boy into paroxysms of grief. (De Quincey, 147–150).

V.1: *Atlantic Ocean water*: Barnabooth had sea water sent to London from Bexhill (*Diary*, 280).

V.7: *Grosvenor Square*: Located in a desirable section of central London.

V.9: *Campamento*: A small town in NW central Colombia, in a once-disputed territory.

V.10: *Arequipa Desert*: In Peru and Chile.

VI.11: *Island of Marken*: Near Amsterdam.

VI.16: *Djürgarden*: The Deer Park, in Swedish. Djürgarden is a large and beautiful park in Stockholm.

VI.20: *restaurants*: There is no exact English equivalent for Larbaud's "*restaurations*," a dialectal Swiss term for "restaurant." In Larbaud's home town of Vichy there was a restaurant called La Restauration, where, as a teenager, he had an occasional beer. We have resisted the temptation to translate *restauration* here as "beer garden." In the first section of "Europe," which takes place on an ocean liner, we translated it as "dining room."

VI.21: *drunken gentlemen*: Similar gentlemen fond of caloric punch, in Copenhagen, are described in Barnabooth's *Diary* (288).

VI.25: *Arsenalsgatan*: In Stockholm, a street near Stromparterren. (See next note.)

VI.27: *Stromparterren*: A square on a little island in central Stockholm.

VI.38: *1905:* We do not know why Larbaud included this date in the 1913 edition but removed those that followed the other sections of *Europe*.

VII.1: *Burlington Arcade*: Known for its expensive shops specializing in men's ties and shirts.

VII.4: *Green Park*: In central London.

VII.6: *Rotten Row*: A fashionable walk along the south side of Hyde Park.

VII.9: *Kensington*: A borough of London.

VII.9: *Johnson*: Dr. Samuel Johnson (1709–1784), English critic, poet, and essayist.

VII.11: *Fleet Street*: In London, a few steps from Johnson's house, and the center of British journalism.

VII.16: *Madame d'Aulnoy*: French countess (c. 1650–1705) and author of *Fairy Tales*.

VII.19–20: These lines recall an image from Wordsworth's 1805 *Prelude* (I.477–78) of a youthful ice-skating excursion: "To cut across the image of a star/ That gleam'd upon the ice..."

VII.26: *Albert Samain*: French poet (1858–1900).

VIII.1: *The greatest of great men*: Frederick the Great, King of Prussia, born in Berlin (1712–1786).

VIII.4: *Moabit*: A workers' residential section in north central Berlin.

VIII.9: *The prince with the nose...*: Frederick the Great.

VIII.14: *Opernhaus Platz*: Opera House Square, in German.

IX.18: *La Chiaja*: An area in Naples, at the turn of the century the fashionable quarter most frequented by foreigners, as visitors and residents. The Riviera di Chiaja is a fine broad street in this area. Larbaud's *Journal*, in an entry dated 29 February 1932, contains this reference to la Chiaja: "This morning, in the via Santa Lucia, a beautiful victoria with two superb black horses at a fast trot, and in the victoria a gentleman wearing a gray hat and a young woman in mourning, slender, delicate, of a perfect elegance. It was a pleasure to see: very Naples of the old days, of 'my time,' like those old men in frock coats and top hats, with their manner and their bearing so patrician, which I happened to see in la Chiaja, on Toledo. For them Naples was still a European capital, like the Hague, Brussels or Lisbon, the capital of the Two Sicilies, not yet entirely assimilated into the Kingdom of Italy" (267–68). The narrator-protagonist of Larbaud's *Mon plus secret conseil* (Pléiade, 699) lunches at a restaurant at the corner of Toledo and la Chiaja.

IX.21: *Kephisia Avenue*: In Athens, leading out to Kephisia, a town nine miles NE of Athens. Like many of Barnabooth's places, Kephisia is a summer tourist and residential area.

IX.22: *Old Phalerum*: Former Cape Kolias, an ancient Greek coastal village on the Phaleric bay. A port of Athens.

IX.22:   *Munychia*: A port near Athens.

IX.23:   *Lesbos*: A Greek island near Asia Minor.

IX.26:   *Sevastopol*: Ukrainian port city on the Black Sea, with good bathing beaches and sanatoria.

IX.28:   *Kirghiz idol*: From Kirghiziya (or Kyrgyzstan), a republic in central Asia.

IX.31:   *Kharkov*: See note for "Images," I.1.

X.7:   *Nereids*: In Greek mythology, the daughters of Nereus and Doris, nymphs of the Mediterranean Sea, personifications of the play of the waves.

X.7:   *Andromeda*: In Greek legend, the daughter of Cepheus and Cassiopeia, king and queen of the Ethiopians, who was fastened to a rock on the shore to bring relief from a flood and the attack of a sea-monster. The Greeks personified the constellation Andromeda as a woman with her arms extended and chained.

XI.4:   *Welschland*: A German term that refers to all those lands where Latin was spoken, that is, the Romance-language countries.

XI.4:   *Romania*: The Roman Empire.

PRIVATE DEVOTIONS, 141

Larbaud told Vincent Milligan (see Milligan's article in the special "Hommage à Valery Larbaud" issue of *La Nouvelle Revue Française*, 5ème année, no. 57) that he had been baptized a Catholic in February or March 1910. Larbaud first revealed his conversion in 1912. In *Private Devotions* this religious shift is recorded, as well as the gradual move away from the persona of Barnabooth toward a more wholly first-person Larbaud (see the note to line 13 of "To Mr. Valery Larbaud"). Near the end of his *Diary*, Barnabooth bids adieu to the diary, to Europe, to his past, even to the French language that he has adopted: "I am even getting out of the way of thinking in French. By dint of talking my native language every day to my family it is becoming my inward language" (315). He also says good-bye to his identity as a writer: "The day when [my *Diary*] appears will be the day when I shall cease to be an author. And I disavow it entirely: it is finished and I am beginning" (314).

The dedication probably refers to Marguerite Caetani, an American woman who founded and edited the literary journal *Commerce* (1924–1932) in Paris, and in the 1940s and '50s *Botteghe Oscure*.

TO MR. VALERY LARBAUD, 143

In the Pléiade edition (but not in the Poésie edition) this poem is "signed" by A. O. Barnabooth, which finally brings into the foreground the elusive Barnabooth–Larbaud dialogue. We have kept the Pléiade signature.

10–11: The Pléiade punctuates these lines slightly differently:

> Dans le soleil et l'air tiède de l'Empire!
>
> —Comme ces poissons rouges de Valbois, par les journées chaudes,

We have followed the punctuation in the Poésie edition.

11:    *Valbois*: The Larbaud family estate, near St. Pourçain-sur-Sioule, between Moulins and Vichy (where Larbaud was born).

13–14: *Arauquarium*: This mispronunciation of "aquarium" suggests that "that man" is South American, and that he is confusing "aquarium" with Araucania, a large territory in Chile, or the Araucanian Indians native to that region, or perhaps the araucaria tree common to Brazil, Polynesia, and Australia. "Arauquarium" also suggests Arequipa, Barnabooth's birthplace in Peru.

WESTON-SUPER-MARE, 147

Weston-super-Mare is an English seaside resort on the Bristol Channel with a long esplanade and a nice view of Wales. Larbaud's story "Gwenny-Toute-Seule" in *Enfantines/ Childish Things* (Pléiade, 519–532) is a recollection of his life at Weston-super-Mare.

The Poésie edition runs together stanzas three and four of this poem to make a ten-line stanza at odds with the five-line stanza structure of the poem. The Pléiade edition has a page break at the crucial point, with no indication of whether or not there is a stanza break. We have divided the long stanza into the more likely five and five.

7:    *guardians of the estuary*: Two rounded outcroppings or holms in the Bristol Channel, Flatholm and Steepholm.

MARSEILLE, 151

2:    *holy Protection*: The main cathedral in Marseille is called Notre-Dame de la Garde, the steeple of which is surmounted by a 30-foot gilded statue of the Virgin that looks out over the entire port and town, the mountains and sea.

EL CID'S VALENCIA, 153

The Spanish hero El Cid captured Valencia in 1094 from the Moors and ruled there until his death in 1099.

1:    *Ay! Mare de Deu, yo no soc valenciá!*: Oh! Mother of God, I am not a Valencian! In Valencian, a dialect that resembles Catalan. Suggested here, also, is *valentía*—the Spanish word for *valiancy, courage, bravery*. Hence it suggests: "I am not brave."

2–3: Since the *v* of *Vos soldats* is capitalized in line 6, we have taken the liberty of capitalizing the phrases in these lines that also refer to the Virgin: *Votre manteau* and *Votre bras*.

6:    *The most cowardly of Your soldiers*: This poem was probably written between 1915 and 1918, when Larbaud lived in Alicante (near Valencia). His desire to work for civilization rather than against it, during the First World War, does not blind him to the possibility of his being "the most cowardly."

7: *Faustina*: Annia Galeria Faustina Minor, known as Faustina the Younger (c. 127–175), wife of the Roman Emperor Marcus Aurelius and a favorite of Roman soldiers at the time.

8: *Mater Castrorum*: Mother of the Camp, in Latin. An appellation given to Faustina as the protectress of soldiers, later a title applied to the Roman Empress.

9: *beautiful lady Brigadier-General*: The Virgin.

10: *imperial tongue*: Latin.

11: *Aixina*: The Valencian term for the *así* of Castilian Spanish: "in this fashion," "thus."

14: *Mientras todos alrededor, como el trueno, gridaban*: "While on all sides, like thunder, they cried out," in Spanish. St. Paul's visit to Ephesus, as reported in Acts of the Apostles 19–20, was the cause of a great uproar among the silversmiths and other craftsmen of the city. Dependent on the industry surrounding the great shrine of Diana and fearful that the gods would be swept away by the Christian movement, they banded together to denounce Paul's presence in Ephesus. This Spanish sentence approximates the description of the uproar as it appears in Acts 19:34.

15: *Magna Diana Ephesiorum!*: Great [is] Diana of the Ephesians! This quotation appears in both Acts 19:28 and 19:34 in the Vulgate Bible. The phrase was chanted by the Ephesian tradesmen in response to St. Paul's presence in the city.

16: *Y cuando Filius Tuus obumbravit super caput meum in die belli*: And when Your Son overshadowed (over) my head on the day of battle, in mixed Spanish and Latin. The *obumbravit* recalls the *obumbrabit* of the Annunciation message ("The Most High will overshadow you"), but the *super* is grammatically superfluous. *Obumbrare* carries the sense of "protect," and is not pejorative.

MILAN, 155

1: *Madonnina gentile*: Kind little Madonna, in Italian. At the highest point of Milan's main cathedral, the Duomo, stands a small gilt statue of Mary, called La Madoninna, the Little Madonna.

3: As in "El Cid's Valencia," in this line we have capitalized the *y* of the word *your*, to keep the capitalization consistent with the other instances of the word in this poem.

4: *Comante Eginetico*: Pseudonym for the abbé Carlo Innocenzo Frugoni (1692–1768), who reigned over literature at the courts of the Farnese and the Bourbons in Parma, and who wrote innumerable poems.

4: *church in Parma*: Probably either the Cathedral of the Assumption or San Giovanni Evangelista.

6–7: *Maria bambina santissima,/Maria santissima, bambina*: Most holy baby Mary,/Most holy Mary, baby. In Italian.

10: *Ambrose*: Ambrose (340?–397) was the Bishop of Milan, later the city's patron saint.

LA NEIGE, 158

This poem, with its theme of snow all over Europe, might have been inspired by an exhibition Larbaud reviewed in his "Letter from Paris" column in the *New Weekly* in 1914, entitled "Les Peintres de Neige" ("The Painters of Snow"): "The idea of exhibiting in the same gallery nearly a hundred snow-landscapes was a good one. There was snow from Canada and from Holland; Spanish and Russian snow had inspired a few French artists, while the snow of Auvergne had caught the fancy of an artist with a Polish name" (London: April 25, 1914, 180). Larbaud wrote his column in English.

Vincent Milligan, in his Columbia University M.A. thesis, *Langues et cosmopolitisme dans l'oeuvre de Valery Larbaud*, says that this macaronic poem, dated Bergen-op-Zoom, 29.XII.1934, and its French translation were originally sent out by Larbaud in 1935 as a Christmas card. The Pléiade and Poésie editions print the macaronic version of the poem with a number of typographical errors; our text follows that of Milligan's copy of the original card, which was published for the first time in his thesis. The macaronic version contains French, Provençal, Spanish, Portuguese, German, English, Latin, and Italian, and was written in a Dutch town that had been attacked and often controlled by the Normans, the English, the French, the Spaniards, and the Germans. Larbaud provided a French translation, which we in turn have translated into English.

SNOW, 159

6: *Carpathians*: Eastern European mountain system.
7: According to the text in Milligan's thesis, this line should read, "Des noirs sapins blanc voile de mariée," rather than the "blancs" of the Pléiade and the Poésie editions.
9: *the Esquiline*: One of the seven hills of Rome.

BIBLIOGRAPHY

Alajounine, Th[éophile]. *Valery Larbaud sous divers visages*. Paris: Éditions Gallimard, 1973.

Brown, John L. *Valery Larbaud*. Boston: Twayne, European Authors Series, 1981.

Commager, Steele. *The Odes of Horace*. Bloomington: Indiana University Press/Midland Books, 1967. (Orig. ed.: New Haven: Yale University Press, 1962.)

Contreras, Francisco. *Valery Larbaud, son oeuvre*. Paris: La Nouvelle Critique, 1930.

Delvaille, Bernard. *Essai sur Valery Larbaud*. Paris: Editions Pierre Seghers, Poètes d'aujourd'hui series, 1963.

De Quincey, Thomas. *Suspiria de Profundis*, in *Confessions of an English Opium-Eater and other writings*. Edited by Aileen Ward. New York: Signet Classics, 1966.

Jean-Aubry, G. *Valery Larbaud, sa vie et son oeuvre*. Monaco: Editions du Rocher, 1949.

Larbaud, Valery. *A. O. Barnabooth, His Diary*, translated by Gilbert Cannan. New York: G. H. Doran Co., 1924; reissued as *The Diary of A. O. Barnabooth*, Kingston, N.Y.: McPherson & Company, 1990; London: Quartet Books, 1991.

———. *Childish Things*, translated by Catherine Wald. Los Angeles: Sun & Moon Press, 1993. English version of *Enfantines*.

———. *Fermina Márquez*, translated by Hubert Gibbs. London: Quartet Books, 1988.

———. *The Hamlet of the Bees*, translated by Alan Bernheimer. Cambridge, Mass.: Whale Cloth Press, 1981.

———. *Homage to Jerome: The Patron Saint of Translators*, translated by Jean-Paul de Chezet. Marlboro, Vt.: Marlboro Press, 1984.

———. *Journal, 1912-1935*. Preface and notes by Robert Mallet. Paris: Éditions Gallimard, 1955.

———. *Oeuvres*, edited by G. Jean-Aubry and Robert Mallet. Paris: Éditions Gallimard, Éditions de la Pléiade, 1989.

———. *Oeuvres complètes*, ten volumes, edited by G. Jean-Aubry and Robert Mallet. Paris: Éditions Gallimard, 1950–1955.

———. *Les Poésies de A. O. Barnabooth*, preface by Robert Mallet. Paris: Éditions Gallimard, Poésie series, 1966.

———. *Poems of a Multimillionaire*, translated by William Jay Smith. New York and London: Bonacio & Saul with Grove Press, 1955. English version of *Les Poésies de A. O. Barnabooth*.

———. *The Translator's Patron*, translated by William Arrowsmith, in *Arion*, new series vol. 2, no. 3. Boston: Boston University, 1975. See *Homage to Jerome*, above, for a different translation of the same text.

Mason, J. Alden. *The Ancient Civilizations of Peru*. Baltimore: Penguin, rev. ed. 1968.

Michelin Green Guide: Italy. London: The Dickens Press, 1965.

Milligan, Vincent. *Langues et cosmopolitisme dans l'oeuvre de Valery Larbaud*. New York: privately printed, 1942.

Newhall, Beaumont. *Latent Image: The Discovery of Photography*. Garden City, N.Y.: Doubleday, 1967.

Mousli, Béatrice. *Valery Larbaud*. Paris: Flammarion, 1998. The first full-length biography.

Weissman, Frieda. *L'Exotisme de Valery Larbaud*. Paris: Nizet, 1966.

Whitman, Walt. *The Complete Poems*, edited by Francis Murphy. Harmondsworth, Middlesex, England: Penguin, 1975.

Wordsworth, William. *The Prelude or Growth of a Poet's Mind (Text of 1805)* edited by Ernest de Selincourt; new edition, corrected by Stephen Gill. London: Oxford University Press, 1970.

See also the Valery Larbaud website at
http://www3.ac-clermont.fr/pedago/lettres/larbaud.htm

TRANSLATORS' BIOGRAPHIES

RON PADGETT's twenty-three books include *How to Be Perfect, You Never Know, Great Balls of Fire,* and *New & Selected Poems,* as well two memoirs, *Oklahoma Tough: My Father, King of the Tulsa Bootleggers* and *Joe: A Memoir of Joe Brainard.* Padgett is also the editor of *The Handbook of Poetic Forms* and the translator of Blaise Cendrars' *Complete Poems* and Guillaime Apollinaire's *Poet Assassinated.* He has collaborated with artists such as Joe Brainard, Jim Dine, Bertrand Dorny, Alex Katz, and George Schneeman. A Chancellor of the Academy of American Poets, Padgett has received Fulbright, National Endowment for the Arts, Guggenheim, and Civitella Ranieri grants and fellowships, and was named Officer in the Order of Arts and Letters by the French government. Ron Padgett lives in New York City. For more information, go to www.ronpadgett.com.

BILL ZAVATSKY grew up in Connecticut and has lived in Manhattan since 1965. He holds B.A. and M.F.A. degrees from Columbia University. He has published two books of poems, most recently *Where X Marks the Spot* (Hanging Loose Press). His co-translation (with Zack Rogow) of *Earthlight: Poems* by André Breton won the PEN/Book-of-the-Month Club Translation Prize. Most recently he was anthologized in *The Face of Poetry* (University of California Press). Zavatsky has received grants in poetry from the New York State Council on the Arts and the National Endowment for the Arts, as well as a fellowship from the Guggenheim Foundation. Twice he has been a fellow at the MacDowell Colony. For many years Bill Zavatsky was the editor-in-chief of SUN Press and *SUN* magazine. He teaches English and film courses at the Trinity School in Manhattan.

EXPOSITION UNIVERSELLE 1900

La Tour Eiffel

TITLES FROM BLACK WIDOW PRESS

TRANSLATION SERIES

Chanson Dada: Selected Poems by Tristan Tzara
Translated with an introduction and essay by Lee Harwood.

Approximate Man and Other Writings by Tristan Tzara
Translated and edited by Mary Ann Caws.

Poems of André Breton: A Bilingual Anthology
Translated with essays by Jean-Pierre Cauvin and Mary Ann Caws.

Last Love Poems of Paul Eluard
Translated with an essay by Marilyn Kallet.

Capital of Pain by Paul Eluard
Translated by Mary Ann Caws, Patricia Terry, and Nancy Kline.

Love, Poetry (L'amour la poésie) by Paul Eluard
Translated with an essay by Stuart Kendall.

The Sea and Other Poems by Guillevic
Translated by Patricia Terry. Introduction by Monique Chefdor.

Essential Poems and Writings of Robert Desnos: A Bilingual Anthology
Edited with an introduction and essay by Mary Ann Caws.

Essential Poems and Writings of Joyce Mansour: A Bilingual Anthology
Translated with an introduction by Serge Gavronsky.

Poems of A. O. Barnabooth by Valery Larbaud
Translated by Ron Padgett and Bill Zavatsky.

Eyeseas (Les Ziaux) by Raymond Queneau *(Forthcoming)*
Translated with an introduction by Daniela Hurezanu and
Stephen Kessler.

Art Poétique by Guillevic *(Forthcoming)*
Translated by Maureen Smith.

Furor and Mystery and Other Writings by René Char *(Forthcoming)*
Edited and translated by Mary Ann Caws and Nancy Kline.

La Fontaine's Bawdy by Jean de la Fontaine
Translated with an introduction by Norman R. Shapiro.

Inventor of Love by Gherasim Luca *(Forthcoming)*
Translated by Julian and Laura Semilian. Introduction by Andrei
Codrescu. Essay by Petre Răileanu.

The Big Game by Benjamin Péret *(Forthcoming)*
Translated with an introduction by Marilyn Kallet.

I Want No Part in It and Other Writings by Benjamin Péret
Translated with an introduction by James Brook. *(Forthcoming)*

Essential Poems and Writings of Jules Laforgue (Forthcoming)
Translated and edited by Patricia Terry.

MODERN POETRY SERIES

An Alchemist with One Eye on Fire by Clayton Eshleman

Archaic Design by Clayton Eshleman

Backscatter: New and Selected Poems by John Olson

Crusader-Woman by Ruxandra Cesereanu
Translated by Adam Sorkin. Introduction by Andrei Codrescu.

The Grindstone of Rapport: A Clayton Eshleman Reader
Forty Years of Verse, Translations, and Essays by Clayton Eshleman
(Forthcoming)

Packing Light: New and Selected Poems by Marilyn Kallet
(Forthcoming)

Forgiven Submarine by Ruxandra Cesereanu and Andrei Codrescu
(Forthcoming)

Caveat Onus by Dave Brinks
Complete cycle, four volumes combined *(Forthcoming)*

Fire Exit by Robert Kelly *(Forthcoming)*

NEW POETS SERIES

Signal from Draco: New and Selected Poems by Mebane Robertson

LITERARY THEORY/BIOGRAPHY SERIES

Revolution of the Mind: The Life of André Breton by Mark Polizzotti
Revised and augmented edition *(Forthcoming)*

WWW.BLACKWIDOWPRESS.COM